The Prison Minister's Handbook

Volunteer Ministry to the Forgotten Christian

John Cowart

Resource Publications, Inc,
San Jose, California

Editorial director: Kenneth Guentert
Managing editor: Elizabeth J. Asborno
Copyeditor: Leila T. Bulling

Reprint Department
Resource Publications, Inc.
160 E. Virginia Street #290
San Jose, CA 95112-5876

Library of Congress Cataloging in Publication Data
Cowart, John L., 1944-
    The prison minister's handbook : volunteer ministry to the forgotten Christian / John L. Cowart.
       p.   cm.
    Includes bibliographic references and index.
    ISBN 0-89390-338-8
    1. Church work with prisoners—United States. I. Title.
  BV4340.C69 1995
259'.5—dc20   95-44869

Printed in the United States of America
00 99 98 97 96 | 5 4 3 2 1

Contents

Acknowledgments

Excerpts from "Prison Chaplain Chisels Out 'Incarceration Spiriutality'" reprinted with permission, *National Catholic Reporter*, P.O. Box 419281, Kansas City, Missouri 64141.

Excerpts from Leonard J. Hippchen, *Holistic Approaches to Offender Rehabilitation*, copyright 1982. Courtesy of Charles C. Thomas, Publisher.

Excerpts from "Getting Involved in Criminal-Justice Ministries" by Charles Meyer, Copyright 1982 Christian Centry Foundation. Reprinted by permission from the May 12, 1982, issue of the *The Christian Century*.

Excerpts from "Religion in Prisons" by W. Rideau and B. Sinclair are reprinted from *The Angolite Magazine* (January/February 1981); Louisiana State Penitentiary; Angola, Louisiana.

Excerpts reprinted from *The American Prison: From the Beginning...A Pictorial History*, 1983, with permission of the American Correctional Association, Laurel, Maryland.

Acknowledgments

Excerpts reprinted from the December, 1990 issue of *Corrections Today*, with the permission of the American Correctional Association, Laurel, Maryland.

| 1 |

The Prison Inmate and Volunteers

My name is Johnny Jones. I am lying in my bunk awake this morning before the rising whistle. I usually wake up before the whistle. There are no curtains on the window and the bright lights from the prison yard illuminate my prison cell, which I share with two other inmates. The cell was designed for only one, but overcrowding has forced prison officials to double or triple up on cell space. I like this time of the day. Everything is quiet, and I have a chance to think.

I am a twenty-one-year-old black male and am serving a fifteen-year sentence for armed robbery. I have been down for three years, and if I'm lucky, with good time, I'll be eligible for parole in a year or two. People on the street might think that I'm a real tough dude. You know, I pulled a gun on a clerk at a convenience store and took thirty dollars to buy some drugs, but I don't think of

1

myself as a really bad guy. I wouldn't go around sticking up old ladies or snatching their purses.

I know, I know. You're going to say I'm making excuses. My volunteer drug counselor has told me making excuses is my old stinking thinking, but I was really down on my luck. Hell, those white collar guys steal millions and get less time than I did. My drug counselor says that's making excuses too. A crime is a crime, you know. I think a lot about that, now.

Since I've been in prison, I've had a lot of time to think. When I got caught, I was real mad at first, but mostly, I was real scared. I'd never been in trouble before—well, not real trouble. I'd been busted for shoplifting and stealing hub caps when I was a juvenile, but this was my first adult conviction. Because I used a gun, I wasn't going to get probation, either. I was going to the penitentiary. I had heard all sorts of horror stories about what happens to young offenders in prison.

I was lucky, though. I made friends right off with Leon. He's older and has done time before, not for anything violent, petty stuff mostly, but he's been through the system and knows his way around. Well, for a few cigarettes a day, he offered to help me. He taught me how to do my time and stay out of trouble, and he was there at my side when trouble did come looking for me. He helped me to get out of a few jams.

As I said, I was real angry about getting caught, but now that I've had time to think about it, it was probably the best thing that ever happened to me. It may sound crazy, but if I hadn't been caught, I'd probably be dead by now. I know I was headed that way. I was hooked on drugs. They were my life and my god. Drugs were all I thought about. In the morning, when I'd wake up, they were the first thing I'd think about. I'd think about where I was going to get the money to buy drugs. Then I'd think about who I would see to get them. Then I'd anxiously get them ready to stick in my arm and drift off on a cloud when I finally got my bump. But since I've been in the joint, I've stopped using drugs. My mind has cleared, and I can think about other things. I could get drugs if I really wanted them. They can be smuggled in through the visiting room, or dropped off at a spot where the grounds detail can find them, or hidden in a delivery vehicle or parcel, or best of all, there are those corrupt hacks to bring them in. Yes, I could get drugs here, but I don't want them, not since I realized it was drugs that got me into prison, and if I was to stay out, I needed to get off drugs. Actually, it wasn't really drugs that got me into prison. My volunteer drug counselor told me I was headed to prison before I ever started taking drugs. He's right, you know. I was already into breaking the law before I ever got interested in drugs. But, now, I'm hooked, and I want to be free.

It was my friend Leon that first told me to start taking my drug classes seriously. Most of those dudes in class don't really want to be there. They just sit through them because they have to. Look, I've watched them. They'll sit there, half asleep, or they'll stare up at the ceiling and twiddle their thumbs and think to themselves, "Oh God, when can this be over," so they can get back to pumping iron, or shooting pool, or playing their criminal games. I was like that until my friend Leon asked me if I wanted to stay out of prison. Well I do, so I started paying attention to what was going on in class.

The teacher really impressed me, too. She is a volunteer. The thing that impressed me about her was the fact that she takes time out of her busy day to spend an hour a week working in the joint. Volunteers are not like the rest of the staff. The staff counselors are paid to be here and deal with us convicts, but the volunteers come in for nothing. I mean they aren't paid by nobody. They come into the joint because they are really concerned about people like me and want to help. And it's not like she's a pansy. She is no pushover. She's well trained and knows how to handle us convicts. I mean she doesn't take no shit off nobody.

Then I met this volunteer in the chapel. He leads a class on spiritual growth, and he began to teach me about God. I'd heard all that stuff before. You know, if you want to get off drugs, you've got to turn on to your higher power. Now, nobody ever says it, but most of us know that the higher power is God. Well, until I met this volunteer, I didn't think too much about God. I stopped being interested in him when I stopped going to Sunday school. Even then, I had a hard time relating to him. You know, he was that old man in the white robe with the long, white beard. He lived in that far away place called heaven and didn't seem to be too interested in us except to make sure we were obeying his rules.

I was sick of rules, and God seemed too much like my old man. When my old man was home, he was always drunk. When I did something that didn't please him, he'd beat the crap out of me. I was real glad when he finally went off and didn't come back. It was my mom who raised us kids. If there was a god, I didn't think he could matter much. After all, he'd given me a pretty sorry start in life, a drunken father, a single parent, poverty, poor education, you name it.

I used to feel real sorry for myself. It gave me a real good excuse as to why I turned out the way I did, but my volunteer drug counselor made me consider my brother. I used to hate him. He always seemed to be so much better than me. He studied hard, did well in school, and stayed out of trouble. Now, he has a good job. I hear he has a nice girl and plans to get married soon. I hated him because he was everything I wasn't. But my volunteer counselor showed me that my brother and I share the same past and have the same roots. While I chose the life of a criminal, he chose to go straight. All of our lives are the result of the choices we make. I am having to live with the choices I made.

But, as I was saying, I met this chapel volunteer who taught spirituality. He talked to me about God. I mean, a lot of people talk about God, but he talks as if he really knows him. God plays a real part in his life, and it shows in the way he acts. He really loves people, and he shows that he loves me. He won't give up on me, even when I want to give up on myself. Like the other day, when I got an incident report. I was caught in an area that is off limits and had to do several hours of extra duty. I was real down on myself, but he told me the story about

> All of our lives are the result of the choices we make.

5

King David. Now, David really fucked up. He fell in love with another man's wife, got her pregnant, and fixed it so her husband would be killed so he could marry her. Now, that's worse than anything I ever did, but he turned to God and showed him how sorry he was, and God forgave him. He gave David another chance. The chapel volunteer shared with me how God had forgiven him, too. He showed me that God forgives me. We prayed Psalm 132, "LORD, remember David in all his troubles" (Cloverdale Bible). God frees me from sin and evil. God frees me from drugs. He helps me to turn my life around.

And that's what I'm doing. I'm getting my life turned around. Oh, I slip up every now and then. I'll say a bad word or catch myself thinking in my old, crooked ways, but I'm really trying to be different, like my friend Leon.

Leon gets out pretty soon. Several volunteers have been helping him in the prerelease program. You know, one of the most difficult times in a convict's life is that time right after he gets out of prison. When you get out, you have a new set of clothes and a few dollars in your pocket, but if you don't have a plan, you won't make it on the outside. The prerelease volunteers help Leon to evaluate his skills and to go after realistic job opportunities. Leon used to want to be a preacher. A lot of inmates want to become preachers. Some do. The volunteers helped Leon to see that his real strengths were in auto repair. He had learned body repair in the prison repair shop and is really good at it. One volunteer has contacted several body shops in the city where Leon lives and has given him some good leads for a job when he gets home. Another volunteer is helping him find a cheap place to live until he can get back on his feet. The prerelease volunteers have taught Leon how to handle money wisely and how to set up a savings account. The chapel volunteers have gotten in touch with several churches where he will live, and their prison ministry teams have already contacted him. His volunteer drug counselor will make certain he is contacted by Alcoholics Anonymous. The chapel volunteers from Prison Fellowship have referred Leon to a Philemon group for former inmates. I bet Leon makes it this time. He's got a plan, and he's got people that want him to succeed. I want Leon to succeed, because if he can make it, I can, too.

I wish the whistle would hurry up and blow, so I can get up. I've got a lot to look forward to today. It's funny that I would say that. Before I became interested in changing, the days here were long and uninteresting, and one day would drag into the next to make a chain of long, uninteresting days. I was just doing time. I guess it would still be like that if it weren't for the volunteers that come into this place.

Take for example the volunteers in the education department. Thanks to them, I've been able to learn to read and do arithmetic and to get my GED. I remember how proud I was when I walked across the stage in the auditorium and the head of the education department put that diploma in my hand. The volunteers that helped me were there, and my mother was there, too. She was so proud. She could see that I had finally decided to make something of myself.

Now, I'm working on some college credits. I want to try to get my associates degree while I'm here. I'm studying really important stuff, like algebra, English literature, and biology, but the course I really like is my drafting class. I always did like to draw, but nobody had the time to encourage me to develop my talent, until now. Now, I'm real good at it. I've gotten a job in the maintenance department. When a project comes up here at the joint, I make the working drawings. My boss is teaching me how to run the computer, and soon I'll be able to do the drawings and work out the cost estimates with the computer instead of by hand. When I get out, I'll have a real trade that will pay good money. But I wouldn't have gotten this far if it hadn't been for that volunteer who first took the time to show me how to use the instruments.

I go to class in the morning and work at my job in the afternoon, but we have free time in the evening. Like a lot of inmates, I've become a real physical fitness nut since I've been in here. I pump iron and run around the track. I think I'm in better physical shape than I've ever been in my life. The volunteers in the recreation department are cool, too. One of them showed me how to set up a physical fitness routine so I get a balanced workout. He taught me how to watch my diet so I eat the right things. They feed us real good here. In spite of what most people think, most of the time, the food is real good and there is lots of it, but there are too many calories. If I'm not careful about what I eat and don't work out, I'd become as fat as a blimp. Some guys do, but I'm not going to let myself become like that.

The recreation department isn't all pumping iron and running the track. One night a week, I take a course in ceramics. I pay for it with the money I make from my job. I've gotten real good at it, too, if I do say so myself. One of my vases was put on display in the visiting room and was sold for fifteen dollars. I used the money to make another vase for my mother. I sent it to her for her birthday.

Other nights, during the week, I go to the chapel. It's a quiet, peaceful place. The chaplain is cool, but I really like the volunteers. I already told you about the volunteer who teaches the class on spirituality, but there is another volunteer who teaches a class about the Bible. I had never read the Bible before I came to prison. When I was first arrested, I tried to read the Bible by myself, but I couldn't understand it. I enjoyed the stories, but I couldn't read very well, and some of the stories didn't make much sense. This volunteer has been teaching us the history of the Bible. She must have studied a lot herself, because she really knows her stuff. Now, I'm beginning to understand all that stuff in Exodus and the prophets. It's beginning to make sense to me, now. I can see that the people in the Bible were real people just like me. They'd mess up and get into trouble, but God would help them out and show them the right way to live.

On Wednesday nights, a preacher man comes to the chapel to lead us in a revival meeting. He's a powerful preacher who preaches with the power of the Holy Spirit. I feel real convicted when he talks, and he encourages me to continue to change my ways and walk with Jesus. We've got a choir, too. Another volunteer comes in to lead that. I'm not much of a singer, but I really enjoy their music. When the choir sings, I join in with all the other inmates in the congregation. Sometimes when I'm walking across the compound, on the way to class or to work, I find that I'm singing one of the hymns. I feel real uplifted and closer to God when I do.

The worst time around a prison is on the weekends. Then time hangs heavily in our hands. There are no classes, and most of us don't go to work. There's nothing to do. Some of us do get visits from our families and friends. My mother comes every two months or so, but it's a hard trip from the city out to where we are. She couldn't come at all except for the bus that one of the churches provides to bring relatives out here to see us. I always look forward to her visits when she comes.

She hates the way she is treated when she does come. The staff often treat her as if she were an inmate. She has to bring her personal things in a plastic purse that the staff can see through. Then she has to walk through a metal detector. Sometimes they pat search her. If it weren't for the volunteers who work in the visiting room, I think she would be afraid to come. They visit with her while she waits for me to come off my housing unit. They reassure her that someone does care about her and that she is still a decent human being. They let her know that she is not alone.

> The worst time around a prison is on the weekends. Then time hangs heavily in our hands.

Some inmates don't get visits at all. Their families live too far away, or else they have given up on them. There is a group of volunteers that work with the chaplain and all they do is visit inmates that don't have any visitors.

Usually on Saturday mornings, I attend a special AA group that meets in the chapel. This group is not like the others. It's strictly voluntary. No one is required to attend. It was started several years ago by a group of inmates that were trying to recover but were tired of the games that most of the inmates play in the required drug classes. They approached the chaplain and asked if they could have space in the chapel to have a meeting. He puts a pot of coffee on for them. At first, they met by themselves, but later, the chaplain arranged to have a volunteer come in from the outside to help conduct the meetings. I go to the meeting every Saturday that I don't have a visit.

If it weren't for the recreation department, weekends would really be a drag. They open up the recreation yard all day Saturday, and they show movies Friday and Saturday nights, but this gets old after a while. I really enjoy the special programs the recreation department provides. These are all provided by volunteers. We often have a group that comes in from the local symphony orchestra. Then there are the drama groups that come in and put on plays for us. The most popular are the rock bands and the country western groups that visit. Sometimes baseball or softball teams will visit and play a game with an inmate team. All of these are welcome diversions from the boredom of the weekends.

Sunday, I go to church. The chaplain provides the Protestant service, but the needs of the other religious groups are met by volunteers.

Catholic deacons bring communion to the Catholic inmates. One does a service in Spanish, another does one in English. They bring musicians with them. Once a month, a priest will visit to hear confessions and to visit the Catholic inmates who are in the prison hospital. I'm not a Catholic, but often I will sit in on their services. Their way of preaching is different than what I get in the Protestant service, but I enjoy listening to what they have to say, and I enjoy singing with them, too. You know, I had never met a Catholic before I came to prison. Now, I have, and I find they are not much different from us Protestants.

The Jews and the Muslims have volunteers who come in to help lead their services, too. Then there are the other religious groups that don't consider themselves to be Protestant or Catholic. These have volunteers that have services for them, too.

Well, the whistle just blew. It's time to start the day. Without the volunteers, this day would not nearly have the promise it holds.

| 2 |

Criminal Justice in Crisis

Johnny Jones is a fictional character, but he is like many prison inmates I have met. They genuinely are sorry for their crimes and the lives they led. They try to change their lives and take advantage of any prison programs that might help them to make it when they get back on the street. The Johnny Joneses of the prison world are like anyone sitting in the pew in church. Without their uniforms, most would look like anyone in the office or factory. They work, they talk, they laugh, they cry. Many of them have done some very bad things, but the majority of inmates are polite and friendly and would probably go straight if given a chance. Unfortunately, even the ones who try to make it are often frustrated by the system. The newspapers are full of stories about former prisoners who have returned to a life of crime.

In February 1989, Carl Buntion was sentenced to fifteen years for sexually assaulting a teenage girl. Fifteen months later, he was paroled. Less than six weeks later, he and his partner shot to death police officer James B. Irby when Irby stopped their car in Houston, Texas.

In 1966 a Texas jury sentenced Kenneth Allen McDuff to death for killing a teenager. His sentence was commuted to life when the Supreme Court banned the death penalty in 1972. He was paroled in 1989. In March 1992, he murdered Melissa Northrup and is suspected in the deaths of several other women. In March 1993, a Fort Worth jury found McDuff guilty of Northrup's death and sentenced him to die by lethal injection.

Curtis Frank Brooks, a convicted rapist, became a born-again Christian while in prison. He was released in May 1990 and seemed to have begun a new life, but in January 1993, he went on a crime spree that lasted for two weeks and stretched across four states. His crimes ranged from kidnapping and sexual assault to car theft and bank robbery. He was arrested in Irving, Texas, after a high-speed chase ended when his car jumped the median of a freeway and crashed into another car, killing the driver. In Brooks's case, the criminal justice system seemed to have worked. Brooks served twice as much time in prison as most people with similar rape convictions and was released only after a special review by the parole board. Before he went on his crime spree, he reported regularly to his parole officer and fulfilled all other obligations of his parole.

People place high expectations on the criminal justice system to protect the innocent and punish the guilty, and they want to blame the system when it fails. The system often fails and mistakes are made, but the criminal justice system consists of men and women who genuinely try to do their best. They must work without adequate evidence and under the pressure of politics, unrealistic budget constraints, and prison overcrowding. The system is a victim of misconceived ideals and shortsighted policies.

Before the 1950s, prisons were seen as places of punishment. Men and women were kept in warehouse-like structures until their sentences were completed. In the middle of the century, this view changed. Prison reformers began to believe that prisons should try to rehabilitate criminals. Many social scientists saw criminals themselves as victims of society's ills: poverty, racial discrimination, poor education, broken families, and alcoholic and abusive parents. While they believed criminals should be punished in order to satisfy society's desire for retribution and to deter others from breaking the law, they thought more should be done. They believed that society was not being served when prisons returned to society criminals who were ill prepared to be model citizens.

Reformers exerted political pressure on prison officials to devise programs to educate, counsel, and train inmates to become productive citizens. While these goals are laudable, they are rarely realized. One example is the Texas Department of Corrections. Four out of five inmates have drug or alcohol depend-

> The system is a victim of misconceived ideals and shortsighted policies.

15

encies, yet the department employs only one drug or alcohol abuse counselor for every thousand inmates. In 1993 the governor and legislature placed an initiative on the state ballot. The people voted to sell bonds in order to construct prison space for one hundred thousand additional inmates. Twelve thousand of these new prison beds are designated for drug rehabilitation. Yet it remains to be seen if future governors or legislators, under pressure to cut spending and hold down taxes, will provide the money to finish the project.

In Texas more than eighty-five percent of inmates are dropouts. Seventh grade is the average educational level, and the majority have an IQ between seventy and one hundred. However, educational opportunities for inmates are limited, and special education is nonexistent. Most inmates leave prison in worse condition than when they arrived. They leave with few vocational skills and are ill-suited to find a job in today's high-tech workplace. Many suffer from the effects institutionalization, which result from living in a tightly controlled environment where all decisions are made for them. Institutionalization dulls inmates' ability to make decisions for themselves and to lead responsible lives in society. Inmates leave with the stigma of being a former felon. They are shunned by society and rejected by many employers because they have a record. They find it difficult to get a job, even if they choose to look for one. It is no wonder that so many return to a life of crime.

In the seventies, the attitude toward prison inmates changed. The nation perceived that rehabilitation was not working, and politicians, in order to alleviate their constituents' fears, turned to a "get tough" approach toward criminals. Sentences became longer and parole was harder to get, but these changes did not solve the problem. Longer sentences and restricted parole actually made life easier for criminals. Prisons, which were already overcrowded, were soon filled far beyond capacity. Federal courts have ruled that the majority of state prison systems are so overcrowded that they violate the United States Constitution's prohibition against cruel and unusual punishment. Federal justices have mandated maximum limits to prison populations, and the states, in order to meet these standards, have resorted to early release for thousands of inmates and have often kept thousands more incarcerated in county jails rather than transfer them to state penitentiaries.

In 1989 alone, the number of inmates in the Massachusetts prison system increased by 820. In order to remain even, the state must construct a new large facility every year (Ajemian 19). Yet, under pressure from angry citizens and panicked politicians, police in many cities have mounted dramatic crackdowns on narcotics sales and drug-related violence. Mark Keiman, former drug policy analyst for the Department of Justice and now a lecturer at Harvard University, says, "What cops produce are more arrests. We've already got more arrests than we can deal with" (Turque 37). The supply of prison beds cannot keep up with the demand. To provide more prison space, authorities in Boise, Idaho, put up the big top. In 1990 nonviolent offenders served weekend terms under a flashy red and white tent ordinarily used for the local fair ("Under the Big Top," *Time* [August 6, 1990]: 29).

In 1977 seventy percent of prison releases were by parole. Ten years later, that number declined to only forty percent (Turque 36). Charles Hargrove, an accused rapist, was freed to make room for Bob Thomas, a petty thief (Hart 98). The result of this "get tough" policy is that fewer people actually go to prison, and those who do get out too soon. Consequently, the length of time criminals spend in prison has declined from eighteen months to one year (Lacayo 29).

In Texas the average prison time served is one month for each year of the sentence. In south central Los Angeles, the word among gang members is to turn yourself in if you're wanted for anything except a serious crime because Los Angeles County's jail system is so crowded that the possibility of a long stretch behind bars is remote (Turque 36). In California criminal defendants turn down offers of probation and choose to go to prison instead. Prisons are so crowded that only the most serious offenders go there, and, when they do, they stand a good chance of getting out in a matter of months; if they receive probation, they will be under supervision for years (Burka 196). Between 1982 and 1987 the percentage of inmates serving six months or less went from eight to forty-four percent (Turque 37). Prison gates have become more like revolving doors; nearly two-thirds of all convicts are arrested within three years of their release. "Prison works to reduce crime only if you don't let the inmates out—ever," says Jerry Miller, a former corrections official who directs the National Center on Institutions and Alternative in Arlington, Virginia (Lacayo 29).

"Corrections used to be a trivial amount of a state's budget," says Barry Krisberg, president of the National Council on Crime and Delinquency, a San Francisco-based advocacy group. "Now states are facing severe choices between more prisons or schools and public services" (Lacayo 30). Education funds in Connecticut have been cut to build and staff more prisons. The University of California system raised tuition for in-state students by ten percent while the 1989 budget for prisons grew by almost thirteen percent. In Ohio the corrections budget grew by twenty-four percent in 1989 while the public school budget grew only two and seven-tenths percent (Barrett & Greene 18).

For every prison bed built, a judge or jury will find someone to fill it. A 1981 study reported that no matter how many new cells are built, they are filled within two years and overcrowded by about thirty percent at the end of five years (Rosenblatt 159). The war on drugs has filled prison beds. Too many nonviolent offenders are in prison filling bed space that should be reserved for violent offenders, who pose real threats to society. In 1984 inmates convicted of violent offenses made up thirty-five percent of the Texas Department of Corrections population. By 1987 only twenty-three percent of the inmates were sentenced for violent acts (Hart 102).

A vicious cycle has been created, and it is spiraling out of control. In an effort to get tough on crime, more police officers are hired and more arrests are made. The resources of already-overcrowded prison systems are stretched beyond their limits. More money is appropriated to build more prisons, which take even more money to manage and maintain. Money is squeezed out of prison rehabilitative programs and public school and university budgets. While prisoners are released unprepared to work in society, public schools fail to prepare students for participation in the workforce, and the spiral goes on. President Clinton has called upon Congress to mandate even longer sentences and hire one hundred thousand more police officers.

Obviously, prisons do not protect society from crime because it is impossible to lock up every criminal. In spite of all the money and effort being spent to control crime, our nation is not safer. Criminal elements threaten to overwhelm the best efforts of lawmakers, civic leaders, and the police. Gangs, drugs, and violence infest our schools and city streets while our prisons fail to punish the offender, deter crime, protect citizens, or rehabilitate criminals. The criminal justice system is in crisis. The "get tough" approach to law and order is a failure. In spite of the angry shouts, we cannot "lock 'em up and throw away the key." It is impossible to build enough prisons to house all the criminals, and it is undesirable to tear down the walls and open the gates.

The natural response is to throw up one's hands and cry that nothing works, but that is not a solution. In spite of its failures, some things in the criminal justice system do work. In the future, criminal justice reform will involve the investigation of new methods, balanced discussion of the problems (without resorting to polemics or ideology), and persistence in the implementation of new methods in spite of the often whimsical nature of public opinion. It is clear that our nation must change its approach to crime and criminals. New ways of thinking must evolve.

Frequently people who have been working on a problem like criminal justice are those least likely to find a solution. Sometimes someone new to a problem will have a much clearer insight and provide the solution. When more people are involved in problem solving, the chance for more feasible solutions is greater. The time has come for ordinary citizens to become involved in criminal justice. "We now need the help of citizens, unhampered by preconceived notions, outworn standards, or other stumbling blocks, to plot a path through all the confusion and error" (Case 19). Citizens who volunteer their time in criminal justice work can bring new and fresh ideas into the system. Through their participation, these volunteers can become the bridge between the system and the community (Case 23). Citizens can express the community's concerns to criminal justice professionals, but they can also express to the community the particular problems faced by the criminal justice system. They can speak the truth in the face of sensationalism and misinformation. If prisons are to change and meaningful reforms are to be established, prisons must have the interest and support of an informed community that is able to examine and question what is done in corrections and to make suggestions on how it could be done better (Case 19). When citizens are involved in prisons, they learn that offenders are people with problems, and the offenders can learn healthy alternatives to crime from the community.

Among the citizens of the United States, Christians provide a unique insight into the nature of humanity and what it means to be human. Christians have a model for what humanity can be and affirm the values of love and forgiveness, which are the foundation stones of rehabilitation. Yet, for the greater part, the church remains aloof regarding the criminal justice system. Unfortunately, most clergy and laypeople do not want to be involved. I have heard many clergy declare that "we should lock them up and throw away the key."

"The fact is that most priests don't want this work," says prison chaplain Father Ted Parker, "though there's tremendous need for them. Usually, if you're involved in 'normally acceptable' ministry, there are many wonderful feedbacks. You don't get that here. You do get people who ask, 'How can you spend so much time with guys who have really, I mean really, hurt people?'" (Jones 14).

Most clergy will not visit their parishioners in jail. It takes time to get a security clearance, and, if they do, it takes even more time to get into a jail, get past all the security checkpoints, and wait until the officers are able to get the inmate from his cell to the visiting area. Many clergy look upon correctional chaplains with suspicion, as "something less than authentic clergy, presumably unfit for the parish" (Pace 397). And while many churches from the fundamentalist right send ministers and laypeople to visit jails and prisons, the mainline churches are absent (Rideau & Sinclair 38).

One example of this occurred at the Angola State Penitentiary in Louisiana. In 1973, the prisoners had to call upon then-Governor Edwin Edwards to intervene with the Catholic church to secure a Catholic chaplain for them (Rideau & Sinclair 37). An inmate at Angola stated, "If I was forced to go to church, I'd pick some other church to go to in here, even though I understand there ain't that much difference between them and the Catholic church. I was born and raised a Catholic, but they cut me loose when I fell in prison. You know, it's like they've showed me what they think of me. What do I look like running behind a church that's gonna cut me loose soon as I get in trouble and don't show no kind of interest in me? They can keep it" (Rideau & Sinclair 39).

This is one inmate's opinion, and it is unfortunate that it singles out one denomination. Most parish communities do not send volunteers into prisons to work with inmates; they ignore the inmates' families, the innocent wives and children who are punished by economic and psychological hardship while their husbands and fathers do their time; and they fail to offer assistance to the released inmates. While Catholics and other churches work outside the criminal justice system for reforms and fight against capital punishment, they fail to get involved "in that nitty-gritty ugly world of prison" (Rideau & Sinclair 56). Most Christians are involved from a distance. They do not provide a ministry that comes close to listen, touch, and be touched by inmates and

> Christians can use their unique insight into human nature and their status as people who are loved and forgiven by God to transform criminal justice.

their families, to be with them where they live.

Christians fail to act because they are afraid, the natural tendency being to think of criminals as despicable, beyond help and hope, unlike the "good" people found in the pew. Christians neglect prison ministry because they, like other people, are caught in the web of hate. The Gospel of Christ is love and not hate. The punishments society heaps upon prisoners out of hate neither alleviate fear nor bring peace (Malseed 6).

The apostle John says that if we say we love God and hate our brother, we are liars (1 Jn 4:20). He also says that perfect love casts out fear (1 Jn 4:18). In this critical juncture in criminal justice, Christians of every denomination are presented with the opportunity to make a meaningful contribution to solve a problem that plagues our society. Christians can use their unique insight into human nature and their status as people who are loved and forgiven by God to transform criminal justice.

While prisons must still exist to protect society, reconciliation can take the place of punishment, and love of the prisoner as a child of God can enable the criminal to change. Norman Carlson, former director of the Federal Bureau of Prisons states,

> All we in the field of corrections can do, and I think
> you can put volunteers in the same situation, is to
> facilitate change. The word facilitate to me means…
> to provide an atmosphere and environment which
> demonstrates care, concern and love for our fellow
> man, an environment that demonstrates our concern
> about them as human beings. We do want to try to
> assist them in every way we possibly can.…The

volunteer is particularly important because you can demonstrate much more than we.... You can demonstrate what society is all about (Kratcoski 33).

| 3 |

A History of
the American Penal System

The United States penal system is a recent development. For most of history, prisons and jails were not places of punishment. Their purpose was to detain prisoners awaiting trial or until their sentence—death, mutilation, branding, flogging, or deportation—could be carried out. Around 450 B.C. the Athenians constructed a prison, which they called "The People's Thing." It was the equivalent of our modern-day death row. In 399 B.C., its most famous inmate, Socrates, was convicted for impiety and corrupting the morals of the young. He was condemned to death, and, in his cell at "The People's Thing," he drank a cup of hemlock. The first known Roman jail was the vast Mamertine Prison, which was built under the main sewer of Rome in 64 B.C. In that prison, the prisoners were confined in cages.

In medieval Europe, prisoners were held within monasteries and abbeys. In twelfth-century England, the Constitution of Clarendon authorized the construction of jails, which were managed by the county sheriffs. They levied high fees against the prisoners, and prisoners were kept in confinement until the fees were paid. Sheriffs often sold food to the prisoners, and inmates without money would go hungry. Similar to New Testament times, prisoners depended on their family, friends, and private charity to provide food and clothing. No attempt was made to segregate prisoners by age, sex, or crime.

In 1779 the keeper of Newgate admitted that most prisoners depended on "money and provisions brought by their friends," though for the "poor and friendless" he provided at his own expense "coarse pieces of meat and made Broth" (Ignatieff 33). The jailers did not subject the prisoners to any discipline or in any way limit their visiting privileges. Without the segregation of prisoners and no attempt to control contraband, all manner of vices and debauchery occurred. The strong and vicious preyed on the weak and defenseless. Women were subjected to abuse at the hands of the male prisoners and jailers. The sheriff's only responsibilities were to keep the prisoners in custody and deliver them to court for trial.

In the eighteenth century, two forces acted together to create a crisis in the British penal system that forced the enactment of dramatic reforms. The first was the Industrial Revolution, which put most of the independent textile workers out of business. Thousands of homeless, destitute craftsmen roamed the countryside. Often these people were driven to petty crimes to support themselves and their families. To deal with the increased crime rate, a series of laws were passed to protect private property and property owners. These laws served to promote a belief that property is more important than people and to force an upper-class sense of values on the poor (Meyer 573).

The Vagrancy Act of 1744 gave magistrates the power to whip or imprison beggars, strolling actors, gamblers, gypsies, peddlers, and "all those who refused to work for the usual and common wages" (Ignatieff 25). The effect of these laws was to strengthen the industrialists' hold over workers. They blocked all exits from the labor market and enforced the full dependence of workers on wage income. The law served to create a labor force dependent upon the wages paid by the shop owners and to remove, as much as possible, supplementary sources of income like petty theft or the taking of game (Ignatieff 26). While the law punished those who could not find employment, it also reduced unemployment by taking thousands of unemployed off the streets.

Banishment was a popular punishment for offenders. Each nation had its place of exile for convicted prisoners: Russia's exiles were sent to Siberia, England's prisoners were sent to the American colonies, and France deported thousands of convicted prisoners to its penal colonies in French Guinea and New Caledonia. Until it was closed after the Second World War, French Guinea's Devil's Island was considered the world's most dreaded penal colony.

The second force that created the crisis in the British system was the American Revolution, which effectively sealed off America from further deportation. Thousands of those under sentence of transportation remained in the county and borough prisons while the government sought other places to send them. Almost overnight, imprisonment was changed from an occasional punishment for a felony into the sentence of first resort for all minor property crimes (Ignatieff 81). With overcrowding, conditions in England's prisons became abominable. The lack of sanitation caused an alarming death rate among prisoners and even threatened the countryside as disease spread from prisons to surrounding towns and villages.

In England the prisons were supposed to be supervised by three outside authorities: the sheriff, magistrate, and grand jury. Yet no one was able to find any act requiring the county and borough magistrates to supervise the keepers, review their expenditures, and conduct quarterly inspections. The first such statue was not enacted until 1791 (Ignatieff 35).

> Almost overnight, imprisonment was changed from an occasional punishment for a felony into the sentence of first resort for all minor property crimes.

The English prison reform was a result of the life work of John Howard. At first, he seemed an unlikely person to begin prison reform. He was a man who wrestled with his conscience in an inner struggle for his salvation. His personal piety was reminiscent of the Quaker traditions of silent prayer, introspection, and faith in the illumining power of God's light (Ignatieff 58). Howard led an ascetic lifestyle. Throughout his lifetime, he rose at dawn, took a cold bath, and after prayers dressed himself "after a style of a plain Quaker." His daily diet consisted of nothing more than "two penny rolls with some butter or sweetmeat, a pint of milk and five or six dishes of tea with a roasted apple before going to bed." He was a "lover of order and regularity" in all his affairs and was particularly noted for strict punctuality and for "the exact and methodical disposition of his time" (Ignatieff 50).

Howard entered politics and secured selection as county sheriff of Bedfordshire. It was as a sheriff that Howard discovered his vocation. Unlike most sheriffs, he took his new job seriously and made regular inspections of the prison. He discovered that acquitted prisoners were detained in prison because they could not pay the discharge fees, and he began to tour neighboring prisons to discover the extent of the practice (Ignatieff 51). He discovered appalling conditions and began a campaign to end the abuses and improve prison conditions.

John Howard wanted to learn more. He toured Europe to study prison conditions and was most impressed by Jean Vilain's Maison de Force (House of Enforcement) at Ghent, Belgium, and the Hospice (asylum) of San Michele in Rome. Vilain was one of the first to develop a system of classification to separate women and children from men and hardened criminals and serious offenders from minor ones. Vilain opposed life imprisonment and cruel punishment; instead he defined discipline by the biblical rule, "If a man will not work, neither let him eat." In Maison de Force, inmates were kept in individual cells and remained silent to meditate upon their sins. The individual cells and silent system used by Vilain were also used at the Hospice of San Michele, built by Pope Clement XI in 1704. The motto of San Michele was, "It is insufficient to restrain the wicked by punishment unless you render them virtuous by corrective discipline" (*The American Prison* 15).

This was the precursor of the modern ideal of rehabilitation of the prisoner. Howard believed a convict's process of reformation was similar to the spiritual awakening of a believer at a Quaker meeting. In the vigil of silence, both the convict and believer hear the inner voice of conscience and feel the transforming power of God's love. Quakers were the first to be attracted to Howard's ideas. Because Howard's ideas closely paralleled their religion, they were drawn to the concept of imprisonment as a purgatory, a forced withdrawal from the distractions of the senses into a silent, solitary confrontation with the self (Ignatieff 58).

> Quakers...were drawn to the concept of imprisonment as a purgatory, a forced withdrawal from the distractions of the senses into a silent, solitary confrontation with the self.

Howard's *State of Prisons* was published in 1777. At any other time, the book would have been dismissed as a "worthy but tedious tract" (Ignatieff 79). Instead, it appeared when the administration of criminal justice in England reached the moment of acute crisis brought on by the American Revolution and the suspension of transportation to the thirteen colonies in 1775. In 1779, the English Parliament passed the Penitentiary Act, which provided for four major reforms: secure and sanitary structures, systematic inspection, abolition of fees for basic services, and a reformatory regime.

Howard's fame rests on the simple fact that he was the first county sheriff to take seriously his obligation to inspect prisons (Ignatieff 36). Howard died of typhus (jail fever) in the Ukraine in 1790, but his legacy lived on in England and in the United States. In 1790 the Philadelphia Society for Alleviating the Miseries of Public Prisons published a pamphlet promoting his ideas. The Society proposed to reform the Walnut Street Jail in Philadelphia and revise Pennsylvania's penal code. The pamphlet's conclusion declared that Pennsylvania should follow England's example and "make our prisons Penitentiary Houses and placcs of correction" (*The American Prison* 31). With the Act of April 5, 1790, the Pennsylvania Legislature made the Walnut Street Jail the first penitentiary in the United States and the world. The Act established the Pennsylvania System, which was distinguished by a philosophy of silence and solitary confinement without work so that prisoners could reflect on their crimes.

The purpose of prison became fourfold: to punish the criminal, to reform the person, to deter crime, and "to remove those persons from society who have manifested, by their tempers and crimes, that they are unfit to live in society" (*The American Prison* 30). As might be expected, solitary confinement began to produce harmful physical and psychological effects on the inmates, and many went insane. To counter these effects, prison officials introduced work, along with moral and religious instruction, as a means of rehabilitation. Religion became the principal effort to apply a definite therapy to the criminal thinking of offenders (*The American Prison* 44). Prison officials appointed chaplains at most prisons and encouraged Sabbath schools and bible classes as well as reading and writing. Religious organizations distributed bibles and held revival services.

The end of solitary confinement did not mean an end of the silent system of discipline. Prisoners were not allowed to communicate with each other. They walked to and from work, meals, or chapel in lockstep so guards could see both hands at all times. At meal times, inmates ate in silence at long tables and sat in the same direction so that each inmate faced the back of the inmate in front of him, preventing communication through hand signals. Inmates were required to stand with their arms folded and eyes downcast when an officer approached. They could not look at or communicate with visitors. Visitation was limited and under strict supervision. The rules also limited communication with the outside world. Letters were censored, and the number of letters an inmate could receive was strictly limited. Prisoners were allowed few, if any, newspapers. Originally, inmates lived in silence in single cells, but they developed ingenious methods of communication such as tapping codes on water pipes. The silent system was abandoned when overcrowding made it necessary to put two or more prisoners in a cell as the prison's population outgrew legislative appropriations for construction.

In the nineteenth century, the American prison system entered an age of expansion. The nineteenth century became the age of the "big house" or the Auburn System.

For reasons of economy, the state prison at Auburn, New York, was built with cell blocks in which cells were constructed back to back in tiers within a hollow building. The doors of the cells opened out onto balconies that were eight to ten feet from the outer wall. This type of prison construction became a unique characteristic of American prisons. Rules and procedures were designed to keep prisoners under total control and emphasized the smooth and undisturbed operation of the prison rather than the reformation of the inmates. Then, as now, prison administrators were judged by the prison's production record and the number of escapes. Sentences were determinate and rehabilitation was not a major concern.

The rehabilitative ideal in America owes its development to a Scotsman in Australia, Captain Alexander Maconochie, and an Irishman, Sir Walter Crofton. Maconochie developed a mark system whereby an inmate could earn freedom by hard work and good behavior. This system facilitated control over the inmate and insured compliance to the rules. Through hard work and adherence to the rules, the inmate could prove his worthiness for early release. Crofton devised a series of stages that guided the inmate's life from the first day of imprisonment to the day of his release. The first stage was marked by solitary confinement and dull, monotonous work. The second stage involved assignment to public works. The inmate moved through a progression of grades until the last stage, when he was assigned to an intermediate prison and worked without supervision and moved in and out of the free community.

The year 1870 was a landmark in the history of American corrections. In that year, the National Prison Congress, which later changed its name to the American Correctional Association, met for the first time in Cincinnati with 130 delegates from twenty-four states, Canada, and South American countries. The keynote speaker was the Honorable A. T. Goshorn of Ohio, who stated, "Granite walls and iron bars, although they deprive the criminal of his liberty and inflict a just physical punishment, do not work that reformation in the soul of the man that will restore him to society regenerated and reformed....It is left to the philanthropic and Christian sentiment of the age to devise ways and means to elevate the unfortunate and wayward to the true dignity of manhood" (Mitford 33). The congress emphasized rehabilitation rather than punishment as the chief mission for prisons. Determinate sentences would be replaced by sentences of indeterminate length. Instead of serving a fixed sentence, prisoners would be released only when they satisfactorily demonstrated that they had reformed.

On the surface, the principle seemed just. The prisoner would not be returned to society until he was completely rehabilitated, but the concept concealed something more sinister. First, prison officials used indeterminate sentences to control inmates. While they claimed to support the humanitarian aims of this system, prison administrators used the sentences to enforce conformity to the prison rules. The inmates were under constant anxiety about being the victims of arbitrary decisions by staff members that could add months or years to their sentences. The indeterminate sentence placed the correctional staff in the position of judge and jury. They had the power to decide what was right for the inmate and punish the inmate if he did not conform.

Second, the system of indeterminate sentences assumed the superiority of a certain set of values and dictated that the inmates learn and accept them. The values usually were those of upper-middle-class, white, Anglo-Saxon, Protestant America. The inmates learned to "play the game" if they wanted to get out of prison. More sophisticated criminals quickly learned to pretend to be rehabilitated and won early releases so they could more quickly return to their life of crime.

Third, inmates serving indeterminate sentences stayed in prison longer. Men committed to prison in 1900 under the indeterminate sentence served an average of six months and twenty-three days longer than those committed in 1890 for identical crimes with definite sentences. By 1906 time served for these same crimes had lengthened by one year, two months, and five days (Mitford 84).

Finally, those who advocated indeterminate sentences assumed that the materials, staff, and training necessary to rehabilitate inmates were provided. The leaders at the 1870 Congress believed all these difficulties would vanish when the administration of prisons was placed in the hands of trained professionals, but in most cases state legislatures were unwilling to provide funds for rehabilitative programs (Mitford 80).

From 1870 to 1900, all of the prisons built in the United States were of the Auburn type. Living conditions were moderately improved by the introduction of ventilating systems. Cells were constructed of steel, and chamber pots were replaced by indoor plumbing and running water in each cell. Most prisons had an education program that included a prison library.

The first half of the twentieth century saw many changes in inmate discipline. Silence was no longer enforced. Negative punishments like corporal punishment were replaced with positive reinforcements, such as parole and early release for good behavior, as incentives for inmates to obey the rules. After the Second World War, changes continued to be made in inmate discipline. The striped uniform and the lockstep disappeared. The most profound change was the expansion of classification as a means to rehabilitation. Inmates were no longer seen as sinners to be saved but as sick persons to be diagnosed and cured (*The American Prison* 148). Classification was an attempt to screen incoming inmates in order to provide them with individualized programs for rehabilitation while they were in prison. Many states developed central reception and diagnostic centers in order to more efficiently use personnel and facilities and to

> Inmates were no longer seen as sinners to be saved but as sick persons to be diagnosed and cured.

insure that the inmates were referred to the proper facility.

Today, classification is seen less as a diagnostic tool for rehabilitation and more as an administrative tool for grouping inmates in institutions according to age, sex, health, tendency toward violence, and risk of escape. Within the institution, classification serves to identify inmates who need basic education, drug and alcohol treatment, and/or psychological counseling and therapy. It also determines the inmate's work detail assignments and is a process for evaluating and reporting on the inmate's progress to the parole board (Hippchen 42).

During the Second World War, psychiatry and psychology were used to assist victims of combat stress. The success of these endeavors encouraged correctional officials try these disciples to help inmates deal with the emotional problems that may have led them into a life of crime (*The American Prison* 200).

The emphasis on the rehabilitation of the criminal led to some serious problems. In addition to the old idea that the criminal must pay his debt to society, the prison inmate was forced into the situation that he must prove that rehabilitation had worked and that he was ready to return to society as a productive citizen. The inmate had to go through a series of humiliating procedures and play by the rules in order to convince prison officials to make good recommendations to the parole board. I know of one inmate with a PhD who was required to get his GED because he had never graduated from high school.

> During their term in a California prison, inmates were led to believe that they would be able to raise their educational level to at least the fifth grade and much higher if they desired, to learn a trade, to have physical defects, disfigurations, and tattoos removed or corrected, and to receive help in various individual or group therapy programs in solving their psychological problems. In effect they were led to believe that if they participated in the prison programs with sincerity and resolve they would leave prison in better condition than when they entered and would generally be much better equipped to cope with the outside world (Irwin 53).

In reality, as inmates were released from rehabilitation programs, they discovered that they were poorly prepared to meet the difficulties of the free world, and they became more and more disillusioned. In 1967 when California inmates were asked what was the main purpose of treatment programs, fifty-five percent agreed that the main purpose was to get more money from the state for more prisons, and twenty-eight percent responded that the main purpose was to control inmates (Irwin 53).

By the 1970s, it became clear that rehabilitation was failing. Indeterminate sentences caused some inmates to spend years in prison for minor offenses because they could not or would not play the game in order to show that they were rehabilitated while other inmates manipulated the system to gain early release, then go out and commit new crimes (Allen 17).

Between 1950 and 1966, more than one hundred riots and other major disturbances occurred in American prisons. After the riot at the State Prison of Southern Michigan at Jackson in April 1952, the American Correctional Association assessed the causes to be inadequate financial support, official and public indifference, substandard personnel, enforced idleness, lack of professional leadership and professional programs, excessive size and overcrowding of institutions, political domination and motivation of management, and unwise sentencing and parole practices (The American Prison 209). In 1992 many state prison systems had not yet addressed these problems. In spite of the emphasis on the rehabilitation of the criminal, most criminal justice officials and members of the state legislatures still regard the primary mission of prisons as punishment, incapacitation of the offender, and the deterrence of crime.

By the end of 1982, the nation's prison population reached a record high of 412,000, compared to 196,000 in 1972 (*The American Prison* 216). In 1989 some 3.6 million citizens lived under some form of correctional supervision. This figure means that approximately one in every thirty-five adult white males, one in every nine adult black males, and one in four black males between the age of eighteen and thirty are either in jail or prison or on probation or parole. About 675,000 citizens were in prison, over 300,000 were in jail, and 2.7 million were supervised in the community under various types of probation and parole programs (DiIulio 3).

Without considering the pricetag, lawmakers reacting to pressure to curb crime enacted longer sentences and sharply reduced the number of inmates eligible for parole. By 1985 all but four states had begun to eliminate indeterminate sentences and to enact some type of determinate sentence with stiff guidelines based on the offender's past and the crime committed. Lawmakers not only wanted to get tough on selected offenders and crimes, they also wanted to make sentencing practices more uniform.

After studies found that parole boards were not able to predict whether prisoners will return to crime when they are released, lawmakers began to curtail their authority. Lawmakers also promoted what is called "truth in sentencing." Judges were required to inform juries how much time a criminal will actually serve for a given sentence. Lawmakers also wanted to make certain that criminals convicted of similar crimes would serve like sentences. Many studies have suggested that similar defendants convicted of similar crimes are serving widely disparate sentences based on geography, race, and the philosophy of the prosecutor, judge, parole board, and others who have a role in deciding prison terms.

Rehabilitation, which prison reformers gave as one of the four reasons a person was sentenced to prison, has been abandoned as unrealistic. The punishment of criminals, the protection of society by the incapacitation of the most dangerous criminals, and the deterrence of others from committing crimes remain (Strasser 38).

Changes in the way prisons are administered have continued, but the pressure to reform has come from inmates. Beginning with the 1970s, inmates unleashed a flood of litigation that challenged almost every aspect of correctional operations: overcrowding, housing, healthcare, recreation, mail privileges, classification, the free exercise of religion, and diet (*The American Prison* 218). However, litigation has not been the only force to produce reform. Reform has also been the response to riots. In the 1970s, a long series of riots mimicked the episodes of the 1950s. The two worst riots took place at Attica State Prison near the beginning of the decade and New Mexico State Penitentiary near the end. In September 1971, a riot broke out at Attica and had a death toll of forty-three, and the New Mexico State Penitentiary riot in February 1980 left thirty-six people dead. Burt Useem, a sociologist at the University of Illinois at Chicago, blames prison riots—including those at Attica and New Mexico—not on sociological factors such as racial hostility but on poor administration (Allen 18).

Questions still remain about the role of prisons in punishing offenders and preparing them for life in the free world. "Having tried 'everything works' and screeched into 'nothing works,' we enter the 1990s in the spirit that 'something works.' Common sense tells correctional workers that exposing offenders to life-enhancing, skills-imparting programs is likely to help keep at least some of them on the straight and narrow" (DiIulio 107). The real answer to prison problems might be strong, fair management and realistic work

> The real answer to prison problems might be strong, fair management and realistic work programs that prepare inmates for the responsibilities of adult life on the outside.

programs that prepare inmates for the responsibilities of adult life on the outside.

Reintegrating inmates into society is still a concern of corrections, but it does not have the importance it once had. Because almost all inmates are eventually released from prison, correctional personnel still attempt to provide inmates with programs that will help them to become productive members of society, but inmate participation in these programs is voluntary. "When inmates were allowed to volunteer for programs, they not only participated in more programs, but they also completed more programs. There were fewer disciplinary problems and fewer assaults" (Waldron & Nacci 5). Prerelease, work release, educational release, work furlough, home furlough, and halfway houses are still used by most prison systems to help inmates work their way back into the community and to keep them from returning to prison. Programs that make use of available human and financial resources in the community, including efforts to provide the offender with non-criminal role models who are realistically within the inmate's ability to achieve (such as employed people who are making it), have in many cases proven effective in reducing recidivism. Other effective programs include opportunities for inmates to enhance their basic problem-solving skills, develop the basic cognitive ability to relate actions to their consequences, build interpersonal relationships, and establish respect for legitimate authority (DiIulio 108).

| 4 |

Modern Prison Settings

Entering any correctional facility for the first time can be a frightening experience. People who enter a jail or prison must get permission. They must present proper identification, and often they must submit to a search. When visitors enter the facility, an officer in a control room opens a gate, the visitors step through, and the gate closes behind them. They will not be allowed to leave until the officers in the control room are certain they are the exact visitors they let enter. A second gate is opened, and the visitors step into the interior of the institution. They are met by their escort, and the gate closes behind them. Around them are walls and barbed wire. Except for the entrance gate, there is no way out. They will be protected by the staff, but the staff is often outnumbered by the inmates by as many as two hundred to one.

Surprisingly, if visitors follow the rules, they will discover that prisons are safer than many of our city streets.

City and County Jails

A jail is a local correctional facility that holds people who are awaiting trial or who are usually serving sentences of one year or less. A prison is a state or federal facility that holds sentenced felons for one year or longer (DiIulio 15). Many cities operate their own jails under the administration of the local police department, while others, like the city of Dallas, Texas, confine their prisoners to the county jail and pay the county a fee for each inmate housed there. Prisoners are transferred to county jails when they are indicted for a violation of a state law. Because of overcrowding, many smaller counties and some cities rent out space in their jails to counties who have a surplus of prisoners. Because jails are designed for short-term confinement, most of them do not provide rehabilitative programs for the inmates. They lack the funds, staff, and space for such programs. Religious services are often held in hallways or gymnasiums. Modern jails, like the new north tower in the Dallas County jail, have space for classrooms and religious services. More effort is being made to provide programs such as AlcoholicsAnonymous, basic adult education, and high school equivalency diplomas to inmates.

The administration of county jails is in the hands of the sheriff. If the sheriff is a capable person or selects professional corrections people to manage the jail, the jail will be well run. However, if the sheriff or his selected corrections people are not capable, the jail will be run poorly and the staff and inmates will suffer unsafe and unhealthy conditions. A jail may be administered by a competent sheriff with a professional administrative staff only to have the sheriff voted out of office in the next election and the administrative staff replaced by political cronies. Recently, the state of Texas passed a constitutional amendment that requires certain criteria for people who seek the office of sheriff.

Federal and State Prisons

Prisons present a special problem to volunteers. Most prisons are in small towns or cities in rural areas, away from large urban areas. Volunteers from urban areas must be willing to travel long distances to visit the prison, and churches in small towns usually have smaller congregations and lack adequate human resources for an effective prison ministry team. Several congregations could join together in prison ministry if ecumenical spirit is good among the churches and members do not allow doctrinal differences to divide them.

Prisons differ from jails in that they are designed for the long-term confinement of individuals. Unlike jails, they are better equipped to provide programs for rehabilitation. Most prisons are the same whether they are federal or state prisons. They have similar staffing and administration. They usually have a wall or fence. Some have watchtowers. They have gates that separate those

47

on the inside from those on the outside. They have guards to watch the inmates and prevent their escape. Prisons are usually classified according to levels of security ranging from low-level camps with no fences or gates and minimal staffing to the high-level maximum security prisons like the Federal Penitentiary at Marion, Illinois, which has three staff members for each inmate.

There are two basic differences between state and federal prisons. The first is in the method of sentencing. In state prisons, inmates usually serve only a portion of their sentence, are allowed time off for good behavior, and serve the rest of their sentence on parole. In the federal system, there are inmates who will be eligible for parole, but criminals who committed their crimes after 1984 serve a straight sentence. There is no parole. Federal inmates are awarded only fifty-four days a year for good behavior. Serving a five-year sentence, an inmate with good behavior will be released after serving four years and three months. On the other hand, in the state of Texas, a typical inmate will serve only five months for a five-year sentence. In Texas, a person serving a life sentence will be eligible for parole after thirteen years, but in the federal system, the inmate will spend the rest of his life in prison. While this practice may help to insure the safety of society, it deprives the inmate of hope.

> The greatest challenge for the prison volunteer who works in the federal prison system is to help the inmate discover hope in a situation where a person will grow old and die behind bars.

The greatest challenge for the prison volunteer who works in the federal prison system is to help the inmate discover hope in a situation where a person will grow old and die behind bars.

The second difference between the state and federal prisons concerns administration. In most state systems, the corrections chiefs, including the wardens, are the governor's appointees and come and go with each change of administration. As in the case of county jails, changes in administration at the governor's level can bring fundamental changes in attitudes and policies to the state's prison system. Such changes in penal philosophy can directly affect the prison system's attitude toward volunteers and their role in the rehabilitative process.

In contrast, the Bureau of Prisons has had only five directors since it was created by Congress in 1930, and about sixty percent of all federal prison administrators began their career as correctional officers (Allen 15). To date, each director has emerged from within the ranks of the prison system without consideration of political party or philosophy. This has produced considerable stability within the Bureau of Prisons. As a product of the Bureau, the director is steeped in its traditions and objectives. Its correctional professionals have developed policies that provide a safe and humane environment for the incarceration of criminals. Even the American Civil Liberties Union, whose National Prison Project has sponsored most major prison litigation, gives the Bureau of Prisons praise (Allen 14). The Bureau of Prisons is a model for prison systems in the United States and around the world.

Managers are rewarded for cleanliness, safety, orderliness, productive prison industries, low staff turnover rate, and no escapes (DiIulio 39).

In many state prison systems, thousands of inmates are idle and do nothing all day except eat, lift weights, and roam around. California alone reported 22,431 idle inmates in 1987 out of a prison population of 65,041 (Allen 8). The administrators of the Bureau of Prisons believe that idleness gives inmates opportunities to get into trouble, so they make certain that inmates are kept busy. Inmates cook all the food, do all the laundry and cleaning, landscape the grounds, staff the libraries, paint, repair and install plumbing and electricity, build shelves and cabinets, and even build and remodel the prisons (Allen 11).

The Bureau of Prisons has a high esprit de corps among its staff. In most state prison systems, the correctional staff (guards) and programs staff (counselors, doctors, and similar personnel) are separate divisions who are often at odds with each other. Every employee of the federal prison system is a correctional officer and gets the same training as the guards. Even chaplains are required to pass a course on correctional techniques, with the exception that they do not take firearms training (Allen 15). Every employee has the responsibility to protect the inmates from harm and to prevent their escape (DiIulio 40).

Critics of the Bureau of Prisons' success cite two popular yet false and misleading explanations. The first is that the Bureau of Prisons has a better class of criminals. Historically, the agency has never held only white-collar offenders. In 1988 forty-six percent of its prisoners had a history of violence, and each year the states transfer many of their most difficult prisoners to the federal system (DiIulio 25). The second explanation is that the federal system spends more money than other prison systems. Actually, the federal prison system spends almost exactly the same on each prisoner as the national average (DiIulio 26).

Juvenile Corrections

The history of juvenile corrections is one of neglect and abuse. Juvenile facilities in both the private and public sectors are often antiquated buildings that offer no privacy, few recreational opportunities, and little or no space for programs. Often the staff is poorly supervised, and children are subjected to severe corporal punishment. The state of Texas was one of the worst until a lawsuit brought the Texas Youth Council under the supervision of the federal court.

On August 31, 1973, Federal District Judge Wayne Justice, in *Morales v. Truman,* handed down a temporary restraining order entitled "Emergency Interim Relief," which determined that the widespread practice of beating and other forms of corporal punishment throughout the Texas Youth Council system, particularly at Mountain View and Gatesville, violated the eighth amendment because it was inflicted in a wholly arbitrary fashion, degraded human dignity, and was unacceptable to contemporary society. He also ruled that juveniles held in custody have a state statutory and a federal constitutional right to treatment (Wooden 17).

Since 1973 little has changed in youth corrections. Professional services such as health and dental care, mental health, or substance abuse programs are only available sporadically. The educational curriculum is often below the standards required by the states for children in public schools. In some cases, juveniles are denied the right to free expression of their religion as guaranteed by the Constitution. In Dallas County, Catholic, Jewish, and Muslim children are not permitted to attend worship services of their own faith but are only provided a nondenominational Protestant service. The laws of most states provide inadequate instructions to administrators and judges to determine which youth are detained, why, and for how long. Yet, in 1989, there were more than 500,000 juvenile admissions to publicly operated, secure juvenile detention centers nationwide, and nearly 100,000 juveniles were admitted to adult jails. More than one half of boys and three quarters of girls were not charged with a serious crime. Thousands are held for months or longer ("Voiceless Children: Juvenile Detention in the U.S.," *Education Digest* 57 [March 1992]: 37).

> Delinquents are thought of as children who have gone astray and need gentle correction to get them back on track to becoming productive adult citizens.

In spite of the abuses, the intention of juvenile corrections is good. Juveniles are not adults, and law and society as a whole still consider them to be children. Delinquents are thought of as children who have gone astray and need gentle correction to get them back on track to becoming productive adult citizens. Hence, the laws governing juvenile offenders are different from those of adults. Juveniles' names are kept from the public. Instead of sentencing, as in the adult criminal justice system, the juvenile is adjudicated in the juvenile court. The language is different in order to symbolize that juveniles are never guilty because they have not completely learned the difference between right and wrong. Rather, the court finds them in need of help and sends them to a reformatory for guidance and treatment. This belief and perception is at the heart of the juvenile justice system (Chaneles 7). In Dallas County, first offenders are not incarcerated but are required to attend counseling with their parents. The widely accepted belief in the juvenile justice system is that community intervention is at least as effective as incarceration (Chaneles 63). Even after the juvenile is placed in detention, if he demonstrates a willingness to work with the treatment specialists and exhibits a desire to change his behavior, he can be released. His crime is removed from the record. However, refusal to change can often result in the juvenile being sent to the penitentiary as an adult after he has turned eighteen.

Many of today's delinquents are members of gangs, and the juvenile justice system attempts to interrupt the juvenile's participation in gang activities. The juvenile is placed in a structured environment. He is required to attend school in a classroom setting and is encouraged to complete his education. In the evenings, he is required to attend group and individual counseling. If the juvenile has a drug problem (and many do—thirty-seven percent of juvenile detainees have used marijuana and ten percent have used cocaine), the detention facility will require the youth to participate in a drug treatment program as well (Dembo et al. 31). Some detention centers provide health and sex education, career education, vocational training, job interview techniques, and consumer education.

As with most criminal justice systems, juvenile justice struggles under a constant shortage of funds. When money is appropriated for the juvenile justice system, it is often absorbed by the operations budget, and little is left for the improvement of programs. There are never enough teachers, parole officers, or caseworkers. At the Dallas County Juvenile Detention Center, there is less than one parole officer for sixty juveniles.

Volunteers can play a critical role in juvenile justice. They can work with parole officers to offer more intense supervision. Unlike the parole officer, they can become a friend to the youth, a role model, and a surrogate parent. Volunteers can also function as teachers in their areas of expertise and can fill in the gaps caused by lack of adequate funding. Volunteers can provide extra tutoring and act as mentors for the youth.

Many juvenile centers attempt to involve parents in the rehabilitation of juveniles. The results of a survey made by the California Department of Corrections show that seventy percent of inmates who remain in contact with their families during incarceration remain arrest-free during their first year of parole (Chaneles 108).

When a child is incarcerated, parents are encouraged to visit; they also participate in an orientation program, which provides them with information about the facilities and what will be expected of their child and what will be provided. Parents are also interviewed by caseworkers in order to provide the staff with information about the child's background and needs. Yet many parents abandon their children. They do not cooperate with the staff and do not visit their children.

Volunteers are always needed to visit these children. They enable the youth to be at ease with another adult without worrying that the staff will use their words against them.

Volunteers who work in a juvenile facility are required to fill out an application and will be screened with a background check and police check the same way they are if they apply to volunteer in any other jail or prison facility. After they have been accepted, volunteers will go through a period of orientation.

Women Prisoners

In the past, women were seen as less culpable than men and were given more lenient punishments. However, in recent history, that has changed. Justice Department statistics indicate that the female prison population rose 21.8 percent from 1988 to 1989, and for nine consecutive years the rate of growth for the population of women prisoners has been higher than that for men prisoners.

From 1986 to 1990, the number of women prisoners doubled to forty thousand (Salholz et al. 38).

In spite of the increase in the female prison population, women's correctional facilities have failed to provide meaningful vocational training. While men are trained for such high-paying jobs as welders and mechanics, women are still taught courses in homemaking or trained for skills in cosmetology or dry cleaning. A woman can leave prison less prepared than a male prisoner to earn an living. Yet, Paul Bestolarides, a program director at the Northern California Women's Facility in Stockton, says women inmates are more motivated about their careers than men are. The Stockton program includes training in landscaping and electrical work (Church 21). In contrast, Malcolm Feeley, director of the Center for Law and Society at the University of California at Berkeley, contends that women inmates have very traditional values and are more interested in marriage and cosmetology ("A Woman Behind Bars Is Often Just Like the Girl Next Door," *Insight* [February 13, 1989]: 13).

Women inmates present a unique problem. One fourth of the women entering prison are pregnant or have recently given birth (Church 21). This is a challenge to correctional administrators. A visit to a prison facility can be a frightening experience for a child. The Georgia Women's Correctional Institution at Hardwick provides a bright, toy-filled visiting room in which inmate mothers may

> One fourth of the women entering prison are pregnant or have recently given birth.

visit with their children (Church 21). In the federal system, a program called PACT (Parents And Children Together) is designed to improve relations between inmate parents and their children. At the Federal Correctional Institution in Fort Worth, Texas, PACT sponsors a children's day when the children of inmates are invited into the prison to visit their parents. The day is filled with games on the athletic field, a haunted house, inmates dressed as clowns, a hot dog lunch with the children's fathers in the mess hall, and a tour of the living quarters. PACT offers parenting advice from professionals in the community on a regular basis.

The problem of pregnancy can be especially traumatic for women inmates. Very often, a woman must complete her pregnancy with little or no gynecological attention and give birth while shackled with handcuffs and leg irons. Fortunately, some institutions provide special housing for women and their babies during the critical months after birth. Rikers Island allows babies to stay with their mothers for up to a year after birth.

Military Prisoners

Military prisoners are like other inmates in that they have committed crimes similar to those committed by inmates in the civilian world. The chief difference between them and other inmates is that they are under the control of the Department of Defense, which manages its own prison system. They are familiar with the requirements to obey orders and respect authority. The Department of Defense maintains a maximum security disciplinary barracks at Fort Leavenworth, Kansas, and several regional correctional facilities at military bases around the country. Military prisoners with sentences longer than three years are sent to Fort Leavenworth, which houses about thirteen hundred inmates.

When members of the armed forces are convicted of a crime by a military court-martial, they are reduced to the rank of private and given a dishonorable discharge. They remain under the control of the military until their sentence is completed even though their enlistment may have expired. In this way, they are caught in a kind of legal limbo. They are not civilians but neither are they on active duty. Some inmates successfully appeal their sentence and return to active duty with their former rank or grade. Those who are unsuccessful are returned to civilian life upon their release.

Military prisoners are afforded many opportunities to prepare themselves to enter the civilian job market. Most military personnel have already received their high school diploma because it is a condition of their enlistment in the armed forces. While they are confined in the disciplinary barracks, they are given the opportunity to receive their associate's degree. They may at their own expense go on to receive a bachelor's degree. Those confined at Fort Leavenworth have the opportunity to learn barbering and receive a license. They can learn silk screen printing and culinary arts. In the prison shops, they can learn plumbing, woodworking, upholstery, carpentry, masonry, machine shop skills, and auto body repair. They can get experience in animal husbandry and horticulture. There is a prison library and a prison band. Some military prisoners are assigned to work release and work for businesses in the surrounding community.

Families of military prisoners have it somewhat easier than those of civilian inmates, at least for a while. Until the inmate's enlistment runs out, the family receives the same benefits as those of other military personnel. This helps to ease the hardship of having a family member incarcerated. However, once the period of enlistment is over, the family is no longer eligible for military benefits. The Department of Defense is attempting to do more for the families of military prisoners.

Military prisoners have the same rights as civilian inmates to practice their religion. Besides the usual services for Catholics, Protestants, Jews, and Muslims, religious services are also provided for those who practice the Native American and pagan religions.

At Fort Leavenworth, between twenty and fifty volunteers work in the religious program. The Bethany Group from the Saint Ignatius Catholic Community at Fort Leavenworth participates in Sunday worship and provides services during the week. Prison Fellowship and the Salvation Army also provide programs during the week. Other groups such as the Church of Christ and the Seventh Day Adventists also minister to the inmates of their faiths. Volunteers who work at Fort Leavenworth attend a Volunteer Ministry Workshop (VMW) in which they are treated to a dinner and then listen to presentations by members of the prison administration. This volunteer orientation keeps volunteers informed about rules and policies that govern inmates and the volunteers' relationship with them. The program is recorded on videotape so that volunteers who enter the program at other times during the year may receive the same training.

Special Lockups

Inmates who are a disciplinary problem, whose classification has not been determined, or who have been threatened by other inmates are usually assigned to a special housing unit called "administrative detention" or "segregation." These inmates, because of their status, may not mix with the rest of the inmate population or participate in programs until their administrative detention ends. These inmates may not participate in religious programs or congregational worship.

In most prisons, the chaplains visit these inmates on a regular basis, and they are allowed religious reading materials. Volunteers are usually not allowed to visit inmates housed in segregation. In some special cases, such as an inmate wanting to receive communion, a volunteer may be allowed to visit the inmate in the special housing unit, but that volunteer must be under the constant supervision of a staff member. Volunteers may be allowed to see these inmates in a special visiting area, but they may not have physical contact with the inmate, and, in some cases, the inmate will be subjected to a strip search after the visit. If you wish to have contact with a prisoner in special housing, you should first seek approval through the chaplain's office.

| 5 |

What Makes a Criminal

Criminals are not just people who have broken the law and serve time in our jails and prisons. They are not people who have been unlucky in life and end up on the wrong side of the law. The life of a criminal is fundamentally different from that of a normal person. Criminals are predatory in nature and have an immature approach to life. They have different needs and a value system of their own.

Criminals see people divided into two classes—those who are predators and those who are prey (Irwin 15). While most people respect society and its laws, the criminal has a general contempt for society and its rules. Most people respect the dignity of individual people and their property, but the criminal sees other people and their property as things to be used.

The criminal's world is a self-centered one. The criminal values other people who do what he wants or can be manipulated into doing so. If the criminal cannot achieve his ends through manipulation, he will resort to stealth, intimidation, or violence. "In crime after crime, he asserts who he is—a singularly special and powerful person with whom the world must reckon" (Samenow 117).

The criminal has an immature personality that seeks to satisfy his need for immediate gratification and excitement. The criminal does not steal to buy food or other necessities for himself or his family but does so to meet these other needs. I once met a young woman from an affluent family. She attended a school system recognized for the high academic achievement of its students. She had a car, wore the latest in fashionable clothing, had jewelry, a television, and a stereo—everything a child could want, and she did not do drugs. When I asked her why she stole, she said it was for the excitement. This young woman is typical of most criminals. The law places a challenge before the criminal. When criminals steal, they must outwit those from whom they steal and avoid detection or capture by the police (Irwin 19). The greater the risk and more narrow the escape, the more exciting the theft becomes and, hence, the more the criminal enjoys it. In many ways, criminals are like children who never grow up (Proelss 72). They are unwilling to set responsible goals for themselves and work toward the accomplishment of those goals. For criminals, having a good time is what life is all about. They cannot comprehend placing obligations ahead of their own convenience or pleasure (Samenow 39).

People who work with criminals in the prison setting see them when they are confined and apparently helpless. When they hear their stories, they are tempted to see them as the victims rather than the perpetrators of crimes that have caused suffering in the lives of innocent victims. Many social scientists have tried to determine how people become criminals and have attempted to prove that the origins of criminal behavior lie not within the person but in the criminal's environment—in slums, poverty, poor schools, abusive parents, criminal associates, drugs or alcohol, and prisons. They argue that until these social evils are removed, crime cannot be eliminated. However, there is a growing school of thought led by Stanton Samenow, a prominent psychologist at Saint Elizabeth's Hospital in Washington, DC, that the causes of crime are not the criminals' environment but the criminals themselves. "Crime resides within the minds of human beings and is not caused by social conditions" (Samenow 6).

Two of the social evils most commonly perceived as causes of crime are poverty and unemployment. However, most poor people struggle to get by through honest means, and they are often the victims of crime because criminals see them as being especially weak. They seek employment in order to alleviate their poverty, and what little they have is taken from them. Frequently, I have sought food or rent money for mothers on welfare who have had

"Crime resides within the minds of human beings and is not caused by social conditions" (Stanton E. Samenow).

their money stolen at gunpoint after cashing their checks.

However, many criminals, by their nature, do not seek employment. Dr. Samenow believes that criminals prefer excitement, and the daily routine of work is uninteresting to them. If they do get a job, it is either to keep from being hassled by their parole officer or to appear respectable; sometimes they use the job to further their criminal career. One criminal boasted he had never worked outside of prison except for a job he got in a safe factory in order to learn about the construction of a certain type of safe and its lock (Irwin 10). Giving a job to a criminal does not change his desire for excitement and self-gratification. "The criminal's most pressing business is crime, not his job" (Samenow 85).

Poor schools are also blamed for the development of criminal behavior. This premise is clearly false. If poor schools caused crime, then one must wonder why all children who are products of poor schooling have not turned to crime. Most struggle against their deficiencies and become respected members of society. I was assigned to a prison that had an unusually large portion of white-collar criminals. The inmate population had doctors, lawyers, accountants, bankers, and ministers. The staff often asserted that some of the most educated crooks in the country were housed there. It was not lack of education that caused them to commit criminal acts; rather their education made them smarter criminals. Instead of using a gun to hold up a convenience store, they used computers to steal from investors. The delinquent is bored by school, and his need for excitement and immediate gratification has little to do with academic learning. A delinquent may drop out of school or, because of social pressure or attendance laws, remain in school to avoid trouble with parents, teachers, and truant officers. Some, like the white-collar criminal, will find in the school curriculum the knowledge to further his criminal career. Often the school dropout will become the astute drug dealer who manages his business as well as an honest retail manager.

While there are abusive parents who often do irreparable harm to their children, most children of abusive parents do not become criminals (Samenow 48). Parents of delinquent children are often the first in a long string of victims. The criminal child engages in a campaign of manipulation, lies, threats, and violence to achieve what he wants. While his parents struggle to cope with his criminal behavior, they are ruined financially while they spend their money on bail, lawyers, court costs, and probation fees. Their marriage is weakened, and their other children often suffer physical and emotional harm (Samenow 26). When they take their delinquent child to therapists, they are often told they are aloof, uncaring, or irresponsible parents (Samenow 35). The child will complain to his therapist that his parents do not understand or trust him and do not want to know his friends. In fact, the child does not give his parents reason to understand or trust him and does not want his parents to know who his friends really are (Samenow 58).

Often peer pressure is cited as a cause of criminal behavior. I have often interviewed young prisoners in jail, and when I ask what got them into trouble, they always respond, "I guess I was just hanging around with the wrong crowd" or "I was in the wrong place at the wrong time." They fail to say that they chose those friends and chose to go with them to the place where the crime was committed. Like other criminals, delinquent children seek excitement and self-gratification and choose to associate with others who share the same values.

Drugs, including alcohol, do not contribute to crime. Many criminologists argue that people use drugs to ease the pain caused by abusive parents, social environment, and their low self-esteem. However, Dr. Samenow states that while criminals may blame their careers on drug use, his research demonstrates that criminals actually began to exhibit antisocial behavior toward their parents, siblings, or classmates and teachers before they turned to drugs. Rather than using drugs because of psychological illness or because of a sense of low self-esteem, criminals begin to experiment with drugs because drugs satisfy their need for excitement and self-gratification, and they use drugs to further their criminal careers. Drugs deaden the criminals' consciences, give them courage, and help them avoid worry about the consequences of their crimes. When they are caught, they try to blame their criminal behavior on drugs in order to get the judge to place them in treatment centers instead of sending them to prison. Often criminals will seek treatment when they real-

> Drugs deaden the criminals' consciences, give them courage, and help them avoid worry about the consequences of their crimes.

ize that drugs are actually a hindrance to their criminal careers.

Finally, prisons do not make criminals. Every person committed to prison was already a criminal. Once in prison, criminals have a choice. They can choose to begin to change their lifestyle and follow a plan to better themselves, or they can continue to live a life of crime behind bars (Irwin 76). Criminals will often make light of their sentences with expressions like, "They gave me three years. Hell, I can do that standing on my head." While in prison, criminals meet new individuals who share their antisocial ways of thought and behavior and teach them new ideas for crime. I have observed many inmates who come to chapel for the sole purpose of meeting their criminal associates. No one forccs the inmate to associate with these criminals and continue the life of crime inside or outside of prison (Samenow 139).

Criminal activity is a choice. Criminals are not the product of their environments. They are the way they are because of the choices they have made.

When criminals land in jail, the first thing they want is to gct out. They havc spent their whole lives trying to manipulate people to get what they want, so it is natural that they will try to manipulate family members, lawyers, district attorneys, parole officers, and judges to get a speedy release.

Once, I overheard this conversation between a prisoner and his attorney.

The prisoner entered the visiting booth and demanded in a loud voice, "Man, you've just got to do something to get me out of here. The food is bad and my girlfriend is about to leave me."

The lawyer replied, "Shut up and listen to me. You're facing twenty-five years to life, so cut out this bullshit and come clean with me."

Prisoners will try to get chaplains or prison volunteers to contact their family, lawyer, parole officer, or judge. They will ask the volunteer to act as a personal reference, even after only one interview, to plead for an early release. Failing to manipulate family or the system, prisoners will turn to God and try to manipulate him, too. They assume the air of religion. They will pray, read the Bible and inspirational literature, organize prayer and Bible study groups, and request the chaplain visit them and pray for them.

On one occasion, a young female prisoner requested a visit from me in order to find Jesus.

"Why do you want to find Jesus?" I asked.

"Well, my boyfriend, who is also in jail, wrote to me that if I found Jesus, Jesus would help me to get out of jail. He says Jesus has made his life so much better."

"Do you think that if you find Jesus, he will help you to get out of jail and make your life better, too?"

"Yes, I do," she answered. "But the trouble is, my boyfriend's been in jail before, and each time he's been in jail, he gets religion."

"Does your boyfriend forget about religion when he is released?" I asked.

"Well, yes he does. As soon as he gets out of jail, he always returns to his life of crime."

"Do you really want to find Jesus?" I asked. "Or do you just want him to get you out of jail?"

"Oh, I want to find Jesus. I don't want to continue to live this way. When I get out, I don't want to come back to jail again."

I counseled her about how to begin a life of prayer that would help her to know Jesus.

Very often the criminal's need for immediate gratification will manifest itself. One young man requested a visit from me.

When asked why he wanted the visit, the prisoner replied, "I want you to pray for me."

"What do you want me to pray about?"

"I want you to pray for me, so I can get Jesus into my life."

"It's going to take much more than that."

"What do you mean?" asked the prisoner.

"It's going to take a lot of work."

"Work?"

"Yes. You have got to pray."

The young man's face fell, and he became dejected. It was as if he wanted me to pronounce the magic words and his life would be changed.

A particular phenomenon occurs among Catholic prisoners before the parole board meets to review the inmates' sentences. The inmates gather in the prison chapel and pray the rosary and the novena to Saint Jude. They encourage each other in their belief that this religious practice will win them an early release. On one occasion, I observed one group of inmates practice this ritual each night until the day the parole board met. When the inmates in this group went before the board, each of them was told to serve all their time. The next day, the prayer service stopped, and many of the inmates stopped attending Mass as well.

Some prison systems offer time off a prisoner's sentence if he participates in religious activities. This plays right into the hands of criminals who will manipulate the system by pretending to be religious.

The prison volunteer wants to help change inmates' lives, but the process is much more complex than offering a few simple Bible verses and a prayer. It is on this point that many of the pastoral counseling methods used by Catholics and the mainline Protestants differ from those of the Evangelicals. The simplistic approach of the Evangelical is to get the inmate to acknowledge that he is a sinner and that Jesus died for his sins, then to accept Jesus as his savior and pray to ask Jesus into his heart. The inmate may have accepted Jesus into his heart, but nothing has happened to change the way he thinks. His motivation is still self-gratification and excitement. The criminals will mask their criminal way of thinking under religious activities.

On one occasion, when I was making my rounds in the county jail, the staff was unusually busy. While I waited, I took out my prayer book and began to pray one of the hours from the Divine Office. When the inmate was escorted into the visiting booth, he noticed the prayer book.

"Chaplain, I really need a Bible like that."

"It's not a Bible. It's a prayer book."

"I really got to have that book. Will you give it to me?"

"No. It is mine, and I need it for myself."

"Come on, Chaplain. I really got to have that book, so I can get saved. Come on, give it to me."

While the inmate wanted to demonstrate that he was religious, he still clung to his familiar criminal behavior. He wanted the book right then, and it did not matter to him that he did not know how to use the prayer book or that it was my own personal copy. The inmate saw the book, decided he wanted it, and proceeded to try to get it for himself.

Another time, I celebrated Mass at the county jail. After Mass, an inmate approached me. He pointed to the corporal, a type of linen tablecloth used in the Mass, which lay on the altar.

"Give me that prayer cloth," he demanded.

"It's not a prayer cloth, but why do you want it?"

"I really do need it. I need it to keep close to God."

In each of these cases, the inmates tried to manipulate me to give them what they wanted. Each tried to make me feel guilty. They implied that by denying their requests, I would prevent them from finding God. In these cases, they saw my property as something they could use for their own gratification.

Often when inmates cannot get exactly what they want, they will become hostile. On one occasion, when I responded to an inmate's request for a visit, the inmate demanded fifty Bibles for the men in his tank.

I responded that Bibles are available on the library book cart, and the next time it came around, he should ask the person pushing the cart to give them the Bibles they needed.

"There aren't ever any Bibles on the cart."

"That's not true," I replied. "The chaplain's office has thousands of Bibles, and they make certain plenty of Bibles are on the cart every day."

"There still aren't any Bibles on the cart when it gets to our tank. All they have is New Testaments."

"I'm afraid that's all we have," I said.

"I've seen other inmates with complete Bibles. Why can't we have any?"

"That's because we get the New Testaments free from the publisher. The county is not allowed to spend public funds for religious items. Everything we give away is donated to us. Occasionally, local churches donate complete Bibles for us to give away. Last week, a church gave us one hundred."

"So why can't we have those?"

"They have already been put on the book cart and given away. One hundred Bibles do not go very far among six thousand inmates."

"Then, you get on the phone to that church and tell them to send fifty more for our tank. Get on the phone, right now, and order those Bibles, or we are going to sue you."

The inmate was not satisfied with what was provided for him; he wanted more at the expense of others. He tried to use the criminal tactic of intimidation, the threat of a lawsuit, to get what he wanted.

One more illustration will show how criminal behavior often masks itself behind religion. I visited an inmate who assured me that he had accepted Jesus. "Jesus has changed my life," he said. He had learned to live peacefully with those around him and had learned patience. The visit was ended, and I went to an adjoining visiting booth to see another inmate. The staff was busy and could not come right away to release the first inmate from the visiting booth and escort him back to his tank. The inmate began to bang his fists against the door of the booth. Then he began to shout. Finally, he repeatedly kicked the door and shouted profanities at the staff.

"The impulses of the men whom we find in prisons are usually crude and aggressive; their minds are undeveloped, twisted, and hostile; their interests are limited and primitive; their tastes, loud and vulgar. Life-goals and life-values are badly distorted, and the inner control mechanisms which permit or prohibit the acting-out of this whole warped world are deficient and feeble" (Proeless 71). Those wishing to enter prison ministry may get the impression from this description of criminals and their behavior that the task is hopeless. Some may think criminals cannot change—so why even try? "The greatest hazard to people working with criminals is not physical attack. More serious is a rapid burnout of enthusiasm, commitment, and interest" (Samenow 248). We might think it better to lock them up, throw away the key, and forget about them—except for Christ. In Christ, we not only have the demand to visit prisoners and to evan-

> "The greatest hazard to people working with criminals is not physical attack. More serious is a rapid burnout of enthusiasm, commitment, and interest" (Stanton E. Samenow).

gelize them, but we must also believe in the innate goodness of human beings. Even the most depraved are capable of conversion and reformation. All are in need of God's love and mercy.

There are times in criminals' lives when they are open to change. These opportunities for change present themselves to criminals during periods of crisis. One of these times of crisis occurs immediately after the time of arrest and confinement to jail. New inmates find their whole social structures collapsing around them. They often lose their jobs. They will worry about what they will do for a living when they are released. Bills are not paid and business goes unattended. Rent is not paid, and cars are repossessed. His relationships with family and friends are severed. Often the families of criminals get so fed up with the criminals' behavior that they break all ties with them. They will not visit or answer letters and will refuse phone calls. "Facing the collapse of his personal world, the eventuality of conviction of a felony and a long prison term, he is very prone to express extreme regret. 'Why did I do it?' 'If only I hadn't done that.' 'Why did I get into this mess?' 'If only I had another chance'" (Irwin 40). Criminals cannot be forced to change. They must reach a point in their lives when they are fed up with themselves and the lives they are living and desire change (Samenow 255).

When inmates seek change, confront them about their criminal way of thinking. Once I encountered an inmate and encouraged him to talk about himself.

After the inmate had told his story, I stated, "It sounds like you have a problem."

"No, I don't have a problem. You're the one with the problem."

"I don't think so," I said. "In a few minutes, I'll leave and go home, but you will still be here in jail."

Another inmate told me, "I just can't understand it. Whenever I go down to Industrial Boulevard, I get into trouble."

Industrial is a rundown area of Dallas with bars, liquor stores, and strip joints.

"Well," I said, "it seems to me that you should stop going down to Industrial."

Inmates will make up excuses to avoid taking responsibility for their actions. One young man, about seventeen years old, told me he got in trouble with the police because his parents threw him out of the house.

"Oh," I said, "so you broke your contract."

The young man bowed his head and admitted that he had a problem with drugs. When he broke his agreement with his parents and his therapist not to use drugs, his parents practiced "tough love" and turned him out into the street.

One inmate related how he had gotten a place to live and a job and had even found a nice girl, but when they had gotten into an argument, he started using drugs and was arrested again. Over a period of several weeks, I counseled him and encouraged him to read the gospels and pray the psalms as a way for God to redirect his thinking from criminal behavior to the way God thinks. The inmate expressed interest in this method of prayer and began to believe his new prayer life was helping him to live a better life.

One day, he was very excited. His girlfriend had come to see him.

"How did the visit go?" I asked.

"Oh, it was great," he said. "I got her to admit that my using drugs again was her fault."

"It wasn't her fault," I said. "She didn't make you start using drugs. When she drove away that night, you were the one who decided to go out and look for some drugs. That was your decision, not hers."

The inmate did not request visits from me again. He did not want to face his own responsibility for what he had done. It was easier for him to blame his girlfriend. The inmate wanted to change, but the criminal has only three paths to choose from: crime, change, or suicide. This inmate, like many other offenders, believed that there is a fourth choice, which is to *appear* responsible but get away with violations on the side (Samenow 255). While volunteer prison ministers are not counselors and should limit their activities to giving spiritual advice and listening, they must be aware of the deception of criminals and not encourage them to get away with it.

Working with criminals is difficult, and, as a prison minister, you should expect setbacks, but do not allow yourself to become discouraged or give up. There are thousands of inmates, and if you fail to reach one, you will find others who genuinely seek help to change their lives. Remember that prison ministry is like fishing. Jesus sends ministers out to become fishers of people. A person who likes

> ...prison ministry is like fishing.

to fish knows that he cannot catch all the fish in the lake, but he hopes to catch a few. Even with the failures, you cannot be certain that no good has been done. It is possible that the young man who blamed his girlfriend for his return to drugs may one day remember what I told him and make a genuine resolution to change the way he thinks.

Have the courage and integrity to point out to inmates the actions that follow the criminal way of thinking. The only role models criminals have followed so far have been other criminals, but you offer the criminal an alternative model: a person who is making it in the free world. By example, you help inmates come to a more mature understanding of how their self-defeating and self-destructive behaviors affect them. To try to diagnose the causes of their criminal behavior or to attempt to treat their condition is not within the scope of your ministry; however, you can guide prisoners in the decisions they are making and help them make choices that do not fulfill their desire for self-gratification or excitement.

| 6 |

A Theology of Prison Ministry

Christians have a long tradition of concern for justice and mercy toward those who are punished and for the care of prisoners. This concern finds its roots in the Bible. The church's present lack of involvement is not in keeping with its tradition or history. Christ did not condemn the woman taken in adultery (Jn 8:10), and he taught not to seek revenge (Mt 5:39-42). He also commanded us to visit those in prison (Mt 25:36).

When Jesus began his ministry, he proclaimed, "The time is fulfilled, and the kingdom of God has come near" (Mk 1:15; see also Mt 4:17). In the Gospel of Luke, Jesus began his ministry by saying:

> The Spirit of the Lord is upon me,
>   because he has anointed me
>   to bring good news to the poor.
> He has sent me to proclaim release to the captives

> and recovery of sight to the blind,
> to let the oppressed go free,
> to proclaim the year of the Lord's favor (Lk 4:18-19).

A new relationship is to be established between God and his people. There will be a new order of justice and punishment based upon God's order and not the order of human beings.

God first proclaimed this new order when he established the kingdom of Israel. The people of Israel were slaves in the land of Egypt, but God set them free and brought them to the promised land with "with fine, large cities that you did not build, houses filled with all sorts of goods that you did not fill, hewn cisterns that you did not hew, vineyards and olive groves that you did not plant—and when you have eaten your fill, take care that you do not forget the LORD, who brought you out of the land of Egypt, out of the house of slavery" (Deut 6:10-12). Freed from slavery in Egypt, the people were to remain free.

Almost from the beginning, this ideal began to break down, and people were held in captivity. Moses detained criminals temporarily until their sentences could be passed. The law could not be enforced without an assurance that the offender would be present to undergo trial (Harvey 82). In Leviticus, a man, the son of an Israelite woman, cursed the name of God. He was "put...in custody, until the decision of the LORD should be made clear to them" (Lev 24:12). In Numbers, when a man was accused of gathering firewood on the Sabbath, "They put him in custody, because it was not clear what should be done to him" (Num 15:34).

When a person owed monetary damages to another and failed to pay, often the debtor was sold into slavery, but even this form of captivity was not intended to be for long (Harvey 82). "If a member of your community, whether a Hebrew man or a Hebrew woman, is sold to you and works for you six years, in the seventh year you shall set that person free. And when you send a male slave out from you a free person, you shall not send him out empty-handed" (Deut 15:12-13).

When Israel established the monarchy, the kings often imprisoned persons whom they saw as a threat to the public order. When Micaiah the prophet predicted the defeat of Israel, Ahab the king had him put in prison and fed on bread and water (1 Kings 22:27). Irijah denounced Jeremiah as a traitor and "imprisoned him in the house of the secretary Jonathan, for it had been made a prison. Thus Jeremiah was put in the cistern house, in the cells, and remained there many days" (Jer 37:15-16).

Later, as Israel was occupied by foreign powers, imprisonment became a familiar punishment. A Roman magistrate could hold a debtor in prison until he paid the last penny (Mt 5:26). For crimes committed under circumstances not covered by Mosaic legislation, the rabbis introduced imprisonment as a judicial punishment.

But captivity, deliberately depriving persons of their liberty, is not supposed to exist in Israel. It is a land of freedom. Slavery and prisons, places of captivity, are not provided for by the Law of Moses. Instead, the Law provided for death by stoning for a grave crime against God or against the accepted morals of society. A small number of crimes carried the penalty of flogging. If

someone injured another, the offender paid the individual he had wronged a sum of money somewhat larger
than the amount of damage he had caused, and the right
relationship in the community was restored between the
affected parties (Colson 66).

The Talmud, which gives insight on how the Law was
interpreted in Jesus' day, taught that judges must do
everything in their power to avoid passing death sentences by rigorously cross-examining the witnesses long
enough to have them contradict themselves or each other
and render their evidence unreliable (Day & Laufer 29).
The Talmud also made it clear that whoever underwent
a judicial punishment such as flogging would not be
visited with any further divine punishment. Even though
the Law said a criminal would not be "guiltless" and
escape the divine wrath, judicial authorities could im-
pose a flogging in order to clear the wrongdoer (Day &
Laufer 30). The "eye for an eye and a tooth for a tooth"
was a law of mercy, which called for forbearance. It was
instituted as a limit on the practice of "blood revenge"
by the offended tribe against the tribe of the person who
had committed the offense and punished the offender
with no more pain than he himself had inflicted. It was
also meant to limit the number of sheep a herdsman could
seek as restitution if one of his animals had been killed
(Day & Laufer 27). The offender restored only what he
had destroyed.

Although the Law was harsh, the punishments of the
Law were imposed with mercy and forbearance. The
prophets Isaiah, Jeremiah, Amos, and others were concerned by economic and social justice and found strict

adherence to the Law offensive when there was unkindness toward one's neighbor. The purpose of the prophets was to inform the people of God's understanding of the meaning of justice (Day & Laufer 36).

People were for one reason or another in prison throughout the Old and New Testament periods, but imprisonment was never considered something normal, and prison was not regarded as necessary to the penal system and the administration of justice. Innocent people might be in prison because of circumstances that were the result of a sinful and disorganized society (Harvey 83).

Jesus begins his ministry by proclaiming liberty to captives and freedom for the oppressed. His mission began the reign of God and restored the peace of the old kingdom of Israel; in the new kingdom of God, captivity will not be tolerated.

> ...he looked down from his holy height,
>> from heaven the LORD looked at the earth,
> to hear the groans of the prisoners,
>> to set free those who were doomed to die
>> (Ps 102:19-20).

> ...who made heaven and earth,
>> the sea, and all that is in them;
> who keeps faith forever;
>> who executes justice for the oppressed,
>> who gives food to the hungry
>> (Ps 146:6-7).

Jesus means more than breaking down the prison walls and opening the gates. In the kingdom of God, a new order exists for his people. The sinful irregularities that have crept into society will be done away at last, and the new kingdom of God will reestablish the peaceful realm where injustice and captivity are no more. In the new kingdom, prisons will not exist because injustice and oppression will be banished (Harvey 83), captives will be released, and those in prison will be set free.

At the time Jesus lived, jailers were paid to keep their charges:

> About midnight Paul and Silas were praying and singing hymns to God, and the prisoners were listening to them. Suddenly, the foundations of the prison were shaken; and immediately all the doors were opened and everyone's chains were unfastened. When the jailer woke up and saw the prison doors wide open, he drew his sword and was about to kill himself, since he supposed that the prisoners had escaped (Acts 16:25-27).

They provided no clothing, sanitation, or healthcare, and the food, if any, was of poor quality. The less they provided for their clients, the greater their profits. The only comforts the incarcerated could obtain were those furnished by family or friends. Often imprisonment was the result of Roman oppression, and good people were expected to relieve those in prison by visiting and other acts of mercy and sometimes by the outright purchase of their freedom. These acts were regarded as meritorious, a *mitzvah*, among the Jews.

The standard lists of *mitzvoth* did not include visiting prisoners, but Jesus often presented a more rigorous standard of righteousness than other rabbis:

Do not think that I have come to abolish the law or
the prophets; I have come not to abolish but to fulfill
(Mt 5:17).

For I tell you, unless your righteousness exceeds that
of the scribes and Pharisees, you will never enter the
kingdom of heaven (Mt 5:20).

You have heard that it was said to those of ancient
times.... But I say to you.... (Mt 5:21ff).

One of Jesus' most dramatic teachings about meritorious
deeds was his parable about Judgment Day.

When the Son of Man comes in his glory, and all the
angels with him, then he will sit on the throne of his
glory. All the nations will be gathered before him, and
he will separate people one from another as a
shepherd separates the sheep from the goats, and he
will put the sheep at his right hand and the goats at
the left. Then the king will say to those at his right
hand, "Come, you that are blessed by my Father,
inherit the kingdom prepared for you from the
foundation of the world; for I was hungry and you
gave me food, I was thirsty and you gave me
something to drink, I was a stranger and you
welcomed me, I was naked and you gave me clothing,
I was sick and you took care of me, I was in prison
and you visited me" (Mt 25:31-36).

Jesus added visiting those who are in prison to the
traditional acts of kindness.

Ministry to prisoners has always been an important
work for Christians. This is made clear in the New
Testament and the history of the early church. St. Paul
writes to the Philippians about "Epaphroditus—my

85

brother and co-worker and fellow soldier, your messenger and minister to my need..." (Phil 2:25). Eusebius, an early historian of the Christian church, reported this about Christians living in the second century. The Christian brothers and sisters in prison were the members of the congregation, the men and women who knelt with the congregation in prayer on Sunday, sang the hymns, and shared the Body of Christ at communion. These brothers or sisters in Christ would not be present in church next Sunday and soon would die. From their Christian charity, the congregation provided for their needs by taking them food, clothing, or a warm blanket. Christian charity compelled the congregation to share their love for their brothers and sisters in prison just as they shared their love with them while they were present, especially now that they were in their final hour.

But Christian ministry behind bars was not restricted to Christian prisoners. Paul wrote, "I am appealing to you for my child, Onesimus, whose father I have become during my imprisonment. Formerly he was useless to you, but now he is indeed useful both to you and to me" (Philem 10-11).

Onesimus, a runaway slave, converted to Christianity while he was in prison. Onesimus, who had robbed his master, returned voluntarily to make amends. Some believe that Christian ministry in prisons and work camps of the Roman Empire had such an impact upon prisoners that the Roman government put a stop to the evangelization of prisoners (Hippchen 387).

Christians did not discontinue ministry to prisoners at the end of the persecutions but continued their work of evangelization to bring prisoners freedom in Christ and hope for a better life. In the Middle Ages, the litany that was recited in solemn processions included, "Show thy pity upon all prisoners and captives," with petitions for other persons in various states of affliction. There was no tendency to call a prisoner a "convict" (Harvey 87). Christians understood that imprisonment was just one of many misfortunes that might befall an individual in this sinful world, and there was no suggestion that prison ministry interfered with the due process of "punishment" that may have been involved in being in prison. In 1488 the order of Misericordin was established to minister to prisoners. Its purpose was to console criminals condemned to death and provide religious services and Christian burial for them (Hippchen 388).

Governments, influenced by Christian teachings, began to replace flogging, brutal mutilation, and other corporal punishment with what was seen as the more humane punishment, incarceration, and the scope of Christian ministry expanded greatly. As its scope expanded, the Christian ministry behind bars soon touched every aspect of the lives of prisoners and laid foundations from which nearly every modern rehabilitation program has risen (Hippchen 388).

> Christians understood that imprisonment was just one of many misfortunes that might befall an individual in this sinful world.

Ministering to prisoners is a thoroughly Christian work. It is commended by the teachings of Jesus, has been faithfully undertaken by the church from its earliest days, and falls into place beside ministries to other victims of misfortune. Prison ministry needs no justification because it is an expression of the basic sense of solidarity with the poor and op-pressed, which is experienced by every follower of Christ (Harvey 87).

Paul says, "Keep in mind those who are in prison, as though you were in prison with them; and those who are being badly treated, since you too are in the body" (Heb 13:3). Everyone is a victim of evil circumstances that result from sin. Prison is just one of these circumstances, and the church's ministry to prisoners is just one expres-sion of Christ's solidarity with the victims of every kind of misfortune. Jesus makes no suggestion that prison ministry is different from other ministries (Harvey 87).

Christians in America are diligent in their response to Christ's call to ministry. They set up soup kitchens and food cupboards for the hungry, supply clothing to the needy, and arrange newcomers' gatherings to welcome strangers to a new community—but they neglect the prisoner.

The central message of the Gospel is salvation from sin and reconciliation with God.

> For God so loved the world that he gave his only Son,
> so that everyone who believes in him may not perish
> but may have eternal life (Jn 3:16).

Christians are challenged by Christ's command to reach out to prisoners with forgiveness and reconciliation.

> As the Father has sent me, so I send you (Jn 20:21).

Christians are called to forgive others as the Father has forgiven them. "For if you forgive others their trespasses, your heavenly Father will also forgive you" (Mt 6:14). Today, as in the days of the early church, the prisoners in America's prisons are members of parish communities, although most are not suffering for their faith (Rothschild 28). Some are there because they chose to perform illegal acts to express their faith or political point of view (Rothschild 30), but almost all inmates are in prison because they stole something or did bodily harm to someone. Often they have stolen from the same parish communities that reach out to help them. They are God's challenge to Christians to go and minister to them with love and reconciliation. Christ is an agent of reconciliation, and each Christian has a ministry of reconciliation to perform (Day & Laufer 42).

Jesus requires Christians to meet the prisoner's bodily and spiritual needs as acts of mercy. "I was in prison and you visited me" (Mt 25:36). "Truly I tell you, just as you did it to one of the least of these who are members of my family, you did it to me" (Mt 25:40). Prison ministry helps prisoners to discover forgiveness, reconciliation, and God's love. They learn that they have not been abandoned by Christ or by Christians and that their spiritual conversion and the freedom that comes from reconciliation can radically change their lives away from alcoholism, other drugs, and crime

> Prison ministry helps prisoners to discover forgiveness, reconciliation, and God's love.

(Hippchen 398). In prison ministry, Christians have a vision of what it means to be human and to be treated humanely. To be human is to be broken and imperfect. To treat prisoners humanely means that Christians treat others as their brothers and sisters (Meyer 575).

| 7 |

Persons Who Influence Your Work within the Prison Setting

Getting to Know the Warden, Associate Wardens, and the Captain

Prisons have been built for custodial purposes, to forcibly hold the criminals whom the courts have turned over to them. Prisons must hold them against their will and in a place where they do not like to stay. The custodial mission of the prison is primary, and when this mission clashes with rehabilitative endeavors like religious programs, custody usually prevails (Proelss 70). In any prison situation, three people stand ready to help or hinder the prison minister's efforts. These persons may have different titles, and, in very small institutions, their roles may be combined and under the direction of one person, but the roles are the same. These people are the warden, associate warden, and captain. The warden may be called a superintendent, and the associate warden may be called a director over the particular area he administers. In jails, the warden's role is often designated as the jail commander. The captain is sometimes called the chief correctional supervisor.

Whatever the title, the prison or jail administration is broken into three or sometimes four basic areas. The warden is the chief executive officer. It is his responsibility to oversee the operation of the correctional facility to which he is assigned. All praise and blame for whatever happens in the institution rests on the warden's shoulders. The warden takes great interest in the volunteers who enter his institution. If they work well, the volunteers help the inmates change their criminal behavior and reform their lives. They also save him many thousands of dollars in services he might otherwise have to contract to individuals in the community. Good volunteers keep the inmates happy. The institution runs smoothly, and the warden and his superiors are happy.

However, volunteers present some risks for the warden. His greatest worry is they will compromise security. The warden worries that volunteers will allow themselves to be compromised by the inmates and with the best of intentions, unwittingly or even knowingly, help the inmates continue their criminal activities by bringing in contraband or organizing an escape.

> The warden's greatest worry is that volunteers will compromise security.

Some volunteers, while seeming to sympathize with the inmates, may become hostages or help to ferment unrest or spark a riot. In any of these situations, the warden and his superiors can become most unhappy. Harm could be done to innocent people outside the prison, thousands of dollars of damage could be done to the institution itself, and there could even be loss of life. If any of these things happens, the warden could lose his job. For this reason, the warden carefully scrutinizes each person who volunteers to work in his institution. He makes certain security checks are made and that volunteers are closely supervised, and he often develops a close relationship with the volunteers, even calling some of them by their first names.

The administration of the prison is divided into two or sometimes three divisions, which are often under the supervision of an associate warden. The most important division is operations. Operations includes everything involving the physical operation of the prison facility: maintenance, budget, personnel, procurement, food service, and corrections. In large institutions, each of these functions will be under an individual department head. The purpose of operations is to provide a safe and humane environment for the inmates and to meet their physical needs.

Working with the Correctional Staff

The correctional staff, the prison guards, is usually under the operations wing of prison administration. Concerning the prison's resources, they are the first priority because the primary duty of the prison officials is to keep their charges locked up and to protect society from criminals committed to their care. The corrections staff will get the money and manpower to accomplish this mission at the expense of all the other departments in the prison. The correctional staff cannot allow any escapes or for the inmates to continue their life of crime while they are behind bars.

For this reason, the correctional staff is suspicious of volunteers and often assumes a position of arrogant superiority over other prison programs and operations. Their first concern is security, and they view all the other staff members and especially volunteers as potential breaches to security. Yet, the volunteer must work with the correctional staff and try to achieve a harmonious relationship with them.

The person rarely seen by volunteers, but often referred to in prisons, is the captain or chief correctional supervisor. He can be responsible to the associate warden for operations or can report directly to the warden on all matters concerning security. He supervises the correctional staff and disciplines inmates for infractions. He is responsible for the integrity of the perimeter wall or fence as well as for all firearms and ammunition. He makes certain all the posts are manned and that all of the prisoners are present and accounted for. He has lieutenants or watch supervisors to assist him in these duties.

> ...the correctional staff is suspicious of volunteers.

You may meet the captain or his lieutenants from time to time. You must obey all the rules and follow instructions and consistently work well with inmates before you can win the trust and respect of the captain and the lieutenants. The captain and lieutenants may seem cold and uncaring, but you should take heart in the fact that many staff members are treated this way. However, as you work within the prison setting and come to know the captain and lieutenants, you will find these men and women to be normal human beings. After winning their confidence, you will find warm companions and close friends in them.

You must be aware that you need to arrive at the prison early and allow time to be processed into the institution. No one comes and goes from a prison at will. Due to shortages in staff or other problems, you may arrive in your designated area late. In spite of this, you must finish your program at the scheduled time. You must be aware that another group may be waiting to use the space. Also, inmates are expected to be at their next assignment on time. They must also be present for counts, meals, and work.

It is not uncommon for the lieutenant to cancel all programs. This can occur when there has been a disturbance, an escape, or inclement weather. You may have just reached the most important part of your material. You must put away the material and wait for instructions from the correctional officers. You can also expect to be interrupted from time to time when correctional officers make their rounds through the facility. They may look into the room to observe that you and the inmates are obeying the rules. The chatter on their radios is almost always disruptive.

Working with Operations Staff

You will often have to work with the personnel department employees. They will be the ones who supervise the security checks and will sometimes interview individual volunteers before allowing them to work within the institution. If you request that prison officials purchase materials for a particular program, you will work through your department head with the procurement office to obtain these materials.

Working with the Programs Staff

The other major division in the prison environment is programs. Programs have to do with the inmates' spiritual, mental, and physical well-being. They have to do with the prisoners' reform and rehabilitation. The major areas covered by programs are inmate classification and unit management, education, psychology, medical, recreation, and religious services.

Inmate classification has to do with identifying the individual's characteristics according to the type of offense and sentence, whether the inmate is violent or nonviolent, and the inmate's escape risk. The inmate is also classified according to his educational level and the work skills he possesses. Some prison systems have diagnostic centers where inmates are housed while they are being classified and before they are assigned to the general prison population. The inmate is then assigned to a housing unit with his own unit team. The team will often consist of a unit manager, case worker, correctional counselor, psychologist, and representative from the correctional staff. The inmate will be interviewed periodically by the team to evaluate his progress toward reform and rehabilitation. The team's recommendations will influence the inmate's parole board.

Working with the Unit Team

You may wish to have interviews with the inmate's unit team members. You may be able to offer insight into an inmate's particular situation in which he may need additional help or counseling, and the team, within the constraints of the Privacy Act, may be able to offer you advice.

Working with Drug Rehabilitation

In some instances, up to ninety percent of inmates can have a dependency on alcohol or other drugs. If they are to lead useful lives in the free world, they must overcome their chemical dependencies. Many drug and alcohol rehabilitation counselors work as volunteers with the psychologists and education department to help inmates turn from drugs or alcohol to more spiritually beneficial pursuits.

Working with Recreation

Many volunteers work with the recreation department in areas as diverse as individual counseling on physical fitness to organized sports activities. Often softball teams from the outside will come into the prison to play inmate softball teams. Inmates are often encouraged to do work that is socially beneficial for the community. In some institutions, inmates are encouraged to join service clubs like the Jaycees. In others, inmates sponsor Special Olympics. Recreation will also provide opportunities for orchestral groups or vocal or dance ensembles to perform for the inmates. Recreation volunteers provide the inmates with positive role models and encourage teamwork and cooperation. They provide a needed spiritual dimension of the inmates' well-being.

Working with Education

In some institutions, the education department is separate from other programs with its own associate warden or director. Many inmates come to prison without the basic skills of reading, writing, or mathematics. Few have completed high school, and most do not have a marketable trade or skill. The education department attempts to help inmates achieve the skills they will need to lead productive lives outside of prison.

Volunteers can work within the prison libraries and teach basic adult education or high school equivalency programs. Others teach skills like computer literacy, metal work, printing, electrical work, and construction trades.

It is not enough to teach an inmate a marketable skill. The inmate must also be able to find work once he is on the outside. Most employers are reluctant to hire a former felon, and this leaves the former prisoner with little hope of finding more than a menial job at minimum wage. The inmate who leaves prison with skills and a good education will soon become discouraged and lose hope when faced with such prospects. Volunteers can be spokespersons to the community to advocate greater tolerance among employers to hire the formerly imprisoned and give them the opportunity to find meaningful employment.

Working with the Parole Officer

If a prisoner does not serve his entire sentence, he is released early on parole. This does not mean the inmate is free. A person on parole is still in the custody of the state and will remain so until the termination of his sentence, be that one year or for life. He is still under supervision and must meet the conditions of his parole. This usually means the prisoner will report periodically to his parole officer, look for employment, pay his parole fees, abstain from alcohol and illegal drugs, and not commit any crimes. Failure to abide by these conditions will cause the parolee to be returned to prison without a trial or hearing. If you minister in a jail, you will often encounter people incarcerated for parole violations. Such inmates will often ask you to find out when they are going to be released. You should not contact an inmate's parole board. The board considers it interference with its business and most likely will not respond to your inquiry. The issue of a parole violator's release from detention depends on the parole board. Since the inmate was on parole, he is still under custody and serving time on his sentence. Even if the inmate is not charged with a new crime, the state can keep the inmate in prison until the sentence is completed. The fact that the inmate failed to comply with the conditions of his parole makes him, in most instances, a less likely candidate for parole in the future.

The most successful parole programs exist where former inmates are closely supervised. Unfortunately, in most systems, the caseload for parole officers is quite heavy, sometimes as heavy as two hundred former inmates. It is impossible for a parole officer to provide close supervision to such a large number. Former inmates who are not closely watched have more opportunities to resort to their former ways.

Some states are experimenting with volunteer parole supervisors. These individuals offer their time to the parole board. After they have been properly trained and determined to be capable of supervising former prisoners, they are assigned one or two parolees. If you enter this type of ministry, you will visit the former prisoner at least once a week at his home and check on all the things that a parole officer does: family life, employment, and the quality of his friends. If a problem results, you will report it to the parole officer, who is then able to take remedial action. Most important, you can become a close friend as well as a counselor and role model. You can be someone the former inmate turns to for advice and help during the difficult period after his release from prison. When he is having trouble finding employment, or when his old buddies come to look him up, or when he is tempted to resort to alcohol or other drugs, the former prisoner can turn to you for support. You and the former prisoner can go have a cup of coffee and talk about the difficulty, which will help prevent the former prisoner from returning to his criminal ways.

Working with the Chaplain

The volunteer working within the religious services or pastoral care department will be under the direct supervision of the chaplain. Sometimes the administrative role of the chaplain is filled by a religious programs coordinator (Hippchen 396), who calls in clergy from the outside world, as needed, to minister spiritual and pastoral care to the inmates (Taft 56). Prison chaplains are responsible for the spiritual well-being of all the inmates. They come to the institution bearing the credentials of their denomination or religion, but chaplains must minister to the religious needs of all. The chaplain must manage a program that facilitates fairly and consistently the exercise of inmate religious freedom (Acorn 98).

The chaplain must see that a Catholic priest is available to hear confessions and celebrate Mass, that Protestant inmates have available a nondenominational service, that Jewish inmates have a rabbi for the Sabbath, and that Muslim inmates have an Imam for Jumah Prayer on Friday afternoon. Chaplains provide for celebrations of Christmas and Easter for Christians, Passover for Jews, and Ramadan for Muslims.

The purpose of these services is to meet at least the minimal requirements of the religious groups. These services require coordination among the minister who works with that particular group, the captain, the food service administrator, sometimes the safety officer, and the warden (Thompson 84). Although the chaplain attempts to meet the constitutional guarantees of religious freedom for all inmates, certain practical and security considerations will not allow every inmate to attend a religious service of his or her own denomination (Thompson 84).

The chaplain must recruit volunteers for prayer groups and Bible studies and provide special services for inmates who do not fall into the traditional categories. Often the chaplain must himself perform security background checks of the volunteers. From time to time, evangelists, music groups, and ministers from other religious groups in the outside world offer to visit the chapel and provide special programs. The chaplain must arrange the security checks of these groups and receive special clearance from the warden for these groups to visit in the prison chapel. When the group arrives, the chaplain must check their equipment for contraband, assist them in getting through the front gate, escort them to the chapel, and supervise them while they are there. When the group is ready to leave, the procedure is reversed.

The chaplain is on call twenty-four hours a day. When a relative of an inmate dies, the chaplain must personally tell the inmate of the death. The chaplain must be ready to console the inmate and follow up during the grieving process (Thompson 84). If an inmate dies, the chaplain must call the family and notify them. If an inmate is in the hospital, the chaplain must visit him.

Chaplains must make regular rounds throughout the institution. They visit the hospital or infirmary, segregation ("the hole" as inmates call it), housing units, food service, prison industries, and any other place inmates might be working. At meal times, the chaplains visit the dining hall to be available for inmates to contact them. On visiting day, the chaplain tours the visiting room to meet the inmates' families and friends and often ministers to personal needs.

The chaplain must also be available to the staff to minister to them in the same way he does to inmates. Staff members often consider the chaplain to be their pastor and will seek him out. The chaplain must attend staff meetings and serve on staff committees. The chaplain must be present at staff social functions.

Finally, chaplains minister to the community outside the prison walls. They carry the message to their religious group and others that all Christians should be concerned for human beings who are incarcerated inside our prisons and jails (Oliver 22).

The ministry of the prison chaplain is extremely difficult. Many clergy look upon correctional chaplains as "something less than authentic clergy, presumably unfit for the parish" (Hippchen 397). Most clergy do not want this kind of work even though the need for them is great. People ask, "How can you spend so much time with guys who have really, I mean really, hurt people?" (Jones 14). While most clergy enjoy the warmth and rewards of parish life, the prison chaplain must wrestle with his ministry.

Joyful events such as weddings, baptisms, and bar mitzvahs play secondary roles in the chaplain's ministry (Acorn 97). Prison chaplains experience a mixture of dedication and disillusionment and must constantly struggle for professional identity within a system that insists that chaplains function as correctional officers while being pastors to the inmates—despite the fact that most of the staff see them as unimportant and officials do not know what to make of them (Taft 54). The ministry of prison chaplains is more demanding than that of parish pastors in many ways. The prison congregation is less homogeneous than the congregations of most pastors, and the chaplain encounters more people with severe problems than is common in most parishes (Hippchen 397). In their ministry, prison chaplains find a double measure of intensity and acuteness of human relationships while they minister in the cell blocks and dormitories of a correctional institution, beside sickbeds, or in the "mental observation" wards of the prison's hospital (Proelss 81).

Prison chaplains will encounter more of those who profess non-Christian and even anti-Christian ideologies than most pastors do. They will normally conduct their ministry in adverse facilities. Fewer than half of the jails served by chaplains in 1973 had offices for the chaplains (Hippchen 397). The chapel is usually shared by all religious groups (Muslim, Jewish, Catholic, Protestant, and various sects). In institutions without a chapel, the room for worship services may be used for a variety of other purposes (Hippchen 399). I have celebrated Mass on the floor of the gymnasium and in a classroom that often has cigarette butts on the floor. The chaplain must schedule religious activities to fit into the overall schedule of the institution, and he competes with other departments for relatively limited space (Hippchen 399).

In a given worship community, there are times when there is little interest in ministering to prisoners (Hippchen 404), and many of the volunteers who do participate in religious programs are often inadequately trained or lack commitment. They soon become discouraged and drop out of the program. Thus, many correctional institutions have a history of on-again, off-again religious programs (Hippchen 403). The prison ministry is not for anyone who wants to see quick and numerous results. Those who bide their time and reflect may see the grace of God

> ...many correctional institutions have a history of on-again, off-again religious programs.

at work, which may not be immediately evident to the casual observer (Proelss 81).

In most jurisdictions, chaplains are required to have some clinical pastoral education and two years of experience in a parish setting (Acorn 98). Seminary work rarely offers opportunities for future clergy to work in a prison setting. Therefore, few clergy come to prison ministry with the necessary specialized training (Malseed 6). Many states and the Federal Bureau of Prisons require their chaplains to participate in security training programs when they are hired by the institution, and chaplains are required to take additional security training each year (Acorn 106). The Bureau of Prisons also requires their chaplains to attend additional courses and seminars to keep their education and training current. However, on-the-job experience is the primary teaching tool for training clergy to be prison chaplains. Sometimes, this experience can be gained under the supervision of an experienced chaplain, but often the chaplain must learn by trial and error and try to profit from his past mistakes.

Learning is important because the prison environment is constantly changing. "Just about the time you think you've learned it, you realize your institution is changing. The kinds of people coming in have changed, or the warden's changed and the new warden has a different philosophy, or you've had trouble and they've tightened up security and now everything is different. So it is a constant relearning process in the institution" (Acorn 98).

Chaplains may work directly for the institution they serve and be paid by that state agency, or they may work for their denomination and be paid by that organization's leaders. In the former case, chaplains are members of the staff and work directly with them. Chaplains are department heads and on an equal level with all other department heads in the institution. Chaplains' ideas, recommendations, and suggestions are considered with the same weight as those of their fellow department heads (Cassler 166). If a problem develops, chaplains can go directly to the staff member involved and get the issue resolved. If necessary, chaplains on staff can appeal directly to policy. Yet, because they are members of the staff, the inmates are suspicious of them and fear they will take sensitive information to the captain. One inmate complains, "Hell, he's just like the rest of them. He's no preacher. He's a policeman. If we had trouble, he'd have a gun just like the rest of the staff" (Taft 57).

If chaplains work for a denomination, they are not staff members and are at the mercy of the staff regarding its interruption of policy. Their ability to get disputes resolved depends on their personalities and how persuasive they can be with the staff with whom they are allowed to interact. Not being on staff, these chaplains may not be allowed to have free access to the inmates as staff chaplains are. Not being on staff, the inmates may trust them more, but the staff will always be suspicious of them. In either case, how well the chaplains get along with the staff and inmates will depend on their particular styles of ministry.

While some people think chaplains too easily adopt the language and agenda of the institutions in which they serve (Malseed 7), chaplains would be a hindrance to a penal institution if they assumed the role of the protective, kind, and sympathetic mother while the remaining members of the staff assumed the role of the stern, disciplinary father. The chaplain is there to see that the institutional program is carried out under Christian principles (Cassler 168). While prison chaplains must listen to the cries of the imprisoned (Malseed 9), they are not on the staff to play "wet nurse" to the inmates but to teach them to do things for themselves in an approved manner (Cassler 168).

Chaplains are often confronted by inmates who have decided that the chapel program is not meeting their needs and demand special privileges. Chaplains are also confronted by groups from the free world who, for one reason or another, think the chaplain is not ministering to the inmates in a proper way and insist that their particular ministry is what the inmates need. In these cases, chaplains must be thoroughly grounded in policy and constitutional law.

The Establishment Clause of the First Amendment prohibits the states from establishing a religion. Inmates cannot be compelled to attend any religious function and inmates cannot use religion to get special consideration with the administration or parole board or to gain special privileges.

> ...chaplains must be thoroughly grounded in policy and constitutional law.

Special housing units or prison facilities for religious inmates is unconstitutional. The Establishment Clause must be balanced against the Free Practice Clause. The state may not prohibit inmates from practicing their religion if the religious practice does not conflict with the secure and orderly operation of the institution. Inmates may attend the religious services of their choice, wear religious garb, possess crosses, rosaries, Bibles, Korans, or other religious material. However, these may be required to be of a certain size or type for security reasons.

If you work with the chaplain, you must follow the rules. Failure to follow them will result in the chaplain's termination of your visiting privilege.

Working with Other Volunteers and Prison Ministries

Like the chaplain, the volunteer working within the prison setting must learn to work with other volunteers and prison ministries. "At times there may be so little interest by a community in ministering to prisoners that an institution will open its doors to any religious group willing to minister within it....On a pragmatic level, a chaplain is most likely to draw upon those religious groups with which he has the greatest contact, with which he feels most comfortable, and that he believes to have the greatest impact on inmate lives" (Hippchen 405). As a consequence, you will encounter many different individuals, each with their own religious agenda. Some, like Jewish or Muslim volunteers, may have been sought out by the chaplain to meet the special needs of some of the inmates. Others are there because they perceive themselves as having some special biblical interpretation that they believe God is calling on them to express to the inmates.

You may find some of the other volunteers openly hostile to your own religious beliefs. Some chaplains are deeply sensitive to the divisions among religious people and will not tolerate literature or remarks that are openly hostile to another's religious tradition, but others will sympathize with the intolerant position and encourage such hostile attitudes. In such cases of adversity, you must persevere patiently in your faith with charity.

You will develop an ecumenical attitude toward other religions. Perhaps for the first time, you will be exposed to the beliefs and practices of Judaism or Islam. Certainly, you will meet a far greater variety of Christian thought than you thought possible. Prison ministry offers opportunities to worship with others and participate in the many rich traditions of faith. A Christian volunteer may be invited to celebrate the Passover or Ramadan. You have the opportunity to celebrate with other Christians the joy of Holy Week and Easter and share the wealth of tradition the different Christian denominations bring to the festival.

You will have the opportunity to work as a member of a team with organizations like Prison Fellowship or Kairos, which work to bring inmates into a closer personal relationship with Christ. These ministries have extensive organizations with well-developed materials and training programs for their volunteers to use with the inmates. Prison Fellowship also ministers to the inmates' wives and children. Prison Fellowship volunteers help prisoners to find self-respect and reconciliation through service projects that selected inmates perform outside the prison. There are ministries like the Gideons, who give Bibles to inmates. The Salvation Army offers Bible studies and assists former inmates in their transition to the free world. Ministries like Chaplain Ray put inspirational materials in prisons. Grace Ministries in Mansfield, Texas, helps inmates find jobs when they are released. In many areas, Catholics participate with inmates in the Rite of Christian Initiation or Cursillo.

Working with Your Pastor and the Church Hierarchy

Whenever possible, you should develop a harmonious relationship with the pastor, bishop, and other church authorities. This is important in several ways. First, church authorities may be able to direct you to other individuals or groups who are ministering in the prisons. This will enable you to share in the experience and expertise of others who may have been working in prison ministry for a long time. Also, working with others in the ministry removes the isolation and provides support during times of stress or trial.

Second, receiving the blessing and approval of the church authorities gives you credibility when working with prison officials. You represent more than yourself; you represent the parish church, diocese, district, or denomination. Some prison officials require volunteers to represent a particular church and be endorsed by the volunteer's pastor. Often, if you encounter indifference or hostility to your ministry, the weight of church authorities can be brought to influence prison officials. Church officials can stand behind you on issues concerning religious practices such as the use of rosaries or receiving holy communion. However, church officials cannot protect you if you violate the rules or prison policy.

Third, the support of the pastor and the church authorities facilitates your ministry to the local church. When you speak to the local church about prison ministry, you will speak with the support of the pastor or bishop. People cannot just ask, "Who are you?" because they know you have the stature of church authorities behind you. This is true whether you are addressing local congregations or church groups about the needs of the prison ministry or trying to go to another parish to enlist the help of people there.

Working with Other Churches

You will work with churches of other denominations. The prison ministry is too large an undertaking for one individual, group, parish, or even denomination. I have found interested persons in many denominations and spoken to groups in many churches to make them aware of the needs of prison ministry and what they can do to help. One church may be able to help with a visitation program while another may be able to work with the families of the incarcerated. One church may have a food pantry, another a clothing closet, and another may be able to provide social services. All of these represent a vast pool of wealth that can be shared in the ministry to the imprisoned and their families.

| 8 |

Ministry to the Families of Inmates

The silent victims of crime are the criminals' families. Often they are the first victims. Mothers, fathers, brothers, sisters, wives, and children have had their money and property stolen to pay for drugs. Parents have spent their fortunes to keep their children out of jail and to pay attorney fees. Wives and children have suffered abandonment or abuse while their husbands and fathers are high on drugs or drunk. They have been forced to live in the secret world of the addict's family, trying to maintain the appearance of respectability while they deny there is anything wrong with the errant family member. When a father or mother is finally arrested and sent to prison, the family bears the additional stigma of being the family of a jailbird. The families stigmatized will often attempt to put greater emotional distance between themselves and the confined family member in order to lessen this sense of degradation (Brodsky 10). The spouse who is left lives a life of isolation and feels betrayed by the spouse who is doing time. The children keep to themselves and do not invite their friends to dinner or to spend the night for fear that someone will find out that their father or mother is a convict.

The families of prisoners suffer in silence, often within arms' reach of the person who sits with them in the pew. When the husband is in jail, the wife finds that she is now the one who must repair the car when it breaks down. She must deal with creditors who cannot be paid. She must worry about the children who misbehave because their father is in jail and is not around to help discipline them. Often she must go on welfare or move in with her parents or a relative. If the offender is the wife, the father must cope with being alone to care for the children. When a single mother is arrested, the children are sent to live with their grandparents or are farmed out to various aunts and uncles.

The relationship between inmates and their families is a key indicator of the extent inmates will become involved with the criminal culture of prison. If inmates maintain strong, positive relationships with their families, they still value objectives and concerns of the outside world. However, if their sole or primary reference group becomes other prisoners, their life objectives, frames of reference, and values systems are likely to become like those of the prison subculture (Brodsky 10). Yet, in many cases, the families of inmates have given up on them and resist any efforts by their convicted relatives to make contact with them. They put blocks on their phones so that they will not be bothered by collect calls from prison, and prisoners' letters go unanswered. Even when families do visit, the family members and inmates fail to communicate with each other. After they have been together for an hour or so, they may spend the rest of the time staring off into space. They do not seem to have anything more to say. They cannot bring themselves to talk about their feelings. Inmates do not want to complain, and families do not want to cause inmates to worry about family problems. Inmates and their families will talk continuously about anything except their hurts, worries, and fears (Brodsky 5). Over time, inmates lose their primary base of support and face a greater risk of failure when they return to the free world. One study indicates that inmates with frequent visits have significantly less parole difficulty than those with fewer visitors. Seventy percent of subjects with three or more visitors were successful in the first year of parole, compared to fifty percent of subjects with no visitors, who were not successful (Brodsky 17). The majority of inmates who fail when they return to the street and reenter a life of crime are those who lack family support.

To be truly effective, prison ministry must also minister to the families of inmates. Many churches reach out to them without realizing the extent of the problem. Too often the family is given some food, clothing, or money without any attempt to minister to

> The majority of inmates who fail when they return to the street and reenter a life of crime are those who lack family support.

117

the souls that are in pain. The prison minister must minister to the needs of the spouse and children with food, clothing, or medical assistance, but he or she must also minister to their spiritual needs. Spouses need the support of someone who will care so that they will not feel isolated. They need support groups in which they can discuss their problems with others who share their pain. Children need the love and acceptance of others so that they will know that they are okay even if their father or mother is not. They need appropriate ways to vent their grief, hurt, and anger, guidance in moral decisions, and help with their schoolwork.

An effective prison ministry will have a group of people in each parish church who are willing to reach out to the families of inmates who live within the precincts of that parish. Church volunteers will visit the family at home. They will help to intervene in any crisis the family may experience. They can provide information on the criminal justice process and help them to locate the proper community service agencies, bear their emotional distress, and plan for the future (Kratcoski 33).

Often the prison minister discovers a family in need through the tears of an inmate who is powerless to help, and the minister must scurry about, making phone calls to various service agencies, in an attempt to find someone who will be willing to help. This stretches the minister's personal resources, and the time he or she spends in these pursuits prevents him or her from ministering to other inmates. This can cause the prison minister to feel isolated and frustrated. If proper parish resources are available, the prison minister can refer the parish ministry team to the inmate's family.

Good security practices dictate that people who work directly with inmates should not have direct contact with the inmates' families. The parish team will be available to the prison minister to receive requests to work with a particular family and, within the limits of confidentiality, report the family's condition to the prison minister. The parish team and prison minister work together to establish a link between inmates and their families. The prison minister can convey the concerns of inmates to the team, and the team can pass along the concerns of the families to the inmates through the prison minister. At the proper time, families can be encouraged to visit inmates and begin to reestablish family ties.

Prison Fellowship is one prison ministry that attempts to work on this model, but there are others. The Salvation Army and the Society of Saint Vincent de Paul of the Catholic Church also reach out to the families of inmates, and others work with inmates' families in various parts of the country. In San Francisco, Connections helps wives of prisoners with transportation for visits. It helps them to find jobs, locate housing, and obtain credit. In South Carolina, the Alston-Wilkes Society reaches out to inmates' families in nineteen counties (Brodsky 5). While the Salvation Army has little contact with the parish churches, and many Catholic churches do not have chapters of the Society of Saint Vincent de Paul, Prison Fellowship attempts to involve all churches at the parish level, and they provide an excellent model for parish churches to follow whether or not they affiliate themselves with that organization. Prison Fellowship does have some doctrinal statements that may be unacceptable to some denominations, but I have found them to be flexible when working with Catholic churches.

Using the Prison Fellowship model, persons at the parish level can provide a forum for families of prisoners to meet and share common concerns. Spouses of inmates can vent their frustrations, offer mutual support, and find strength in prayer and the sharing of Scripture.

Inmates may have done their share to rupture family ties, but the prison system does little to encourage the reconciliation of them. Often the first correspondence that male inmates receive from their wives are "Dear John" letters or letters from their wives' attornies. Prison Fellowship attempts to counter the destructive forces of incarceration with marriage enrichment seminars. Usually held in the visiting room when it is not being used, the seminars are conducted by married couples who have survived the stress of incarceration by one spouse. The couples share their experiences with the inmates and their spouses and encourage them to begin meaningful dialogue about their problems, hurts, and feelings.

Children feel an especial loss when a parent is in prison. They are often told that mommy or daddy is in the hospital or away on a long trip. When they are told the truth, they fail to understand the meaning of incarceration. They feel abandoned by the missing parent and often express these feelings by bed wetting, sickness, misbehavior, and low achievement in school (Brodsky 13). Prisons are usually far away from the place where the children live, so they do not get to visit often, if at all. When they do visit, they must compete with the adults and other siblings for the attention of the parent in the brief time that is available for the visit. Most visiting rooms are uncomfortable and noisy. Visitors are not allowed to bring food with them and must purchase snacks from a vending machine. The end of the visiting period and departure can be heartrending as the child is often literally torn screaming from the parent's arms.

Some prison systems attempt to make visiting more pleasant for children. The Federal Bureau of Prisons provides special rooms, filled with toys, where children and their inmate parents can visit together. The visiting yard will have playground equipment. Parents and Children Together (PACT) volunteers teach inmates classes on parenting and child rearing. Often they will raise money for transportation so that children of inmate parents can come for a visit.

Prison Fellowship and the Salvation Army help to enforce the bond between parent and child with the Angel Tree program, which distributes toys to the children of inmates at Christmas. Inmates with children fill out a request form on which they list their children, their sexes and ages, and their address. Volunteers then put the children's names on paper angels, which are distributed to local churches. Church members are requested to take an angel, purchase a toy for that child, and send it to the child in the name of the child's parent. The Seventh Day Adventists provide scholarships to the children of incarcerated parents so they can attend one of their summer camps.

Children of inmates often become delinquent because they feel rejected by their parents and ignored by their troubled families. Prison authorities and volunteers who work with the children of inmates have a responsibility to try to prevent the children of inmate parents from becoming another generation of criminals. Volunteers have a responsibility to show the children of inmates that although their mother or father may be in prison, the rest of the world does not hold them responsible and respects them with love and concern.

| 9 |

Special Ministries

Ministry to Incarcerated Juveniles

As noted in chapter 4, juvenile offenders are considered to be children who need help rather than criminals who need punishment. A youthful offender is sent to a juvenile facility in order to receive treatment, and the youth's response to treatment determines how long the youth will remain at the facility.

However, increasing involvement by juveniles in gang activities has begun to change the way law enforcement agencies treat juvenile crime. The problem is how to deal with violent youthful offenders who are too criminal to be juveniles and too young to be criminals (Chaneles 6). Today, there is little difference between the juvenile offender and the adult offender, and often juveniles will be detained at a juvenile facility only long enough for them to reach the age when they can be classified as adult offenders.

Gangs offer juvenile offenders certain status they fail to receive from more socially acceptable forms of behavior. The most important of these are the need to belong and the need for protection. While gangs meet these needs, they also involve the youth in criminal activities like auto theft, drugs, and violence. Frequently these gang affiliations carry over into the offenders' lives as adults.

Admission to a juvenile facility puts youths under a high degree of stress. Juvenile offenders have to learn a whole new way of thinking. They have to learn and understand the language, people, and customs that constitute the inmate culture. They must also learn to deal with authority. Though a youth may have been regarded as the "toughest of the tough" by his peers on the street, he must now put up with being "bossed around" by the older inmates and staff. Youths must also learn to deal with restricted space. "Space" is more than the confined space of the facility; it is also "bargaining space," which is the ability to negotiate and make one's point with the other inmates and with the staff (Chaneles 10). Membership in a gang helps inmates deal with these problems. When inmates are members of a gang, they have allies who can teach them the way of incarcerated life and help them deal with hostile inmates. Inmates who are gang members hang out together in the institution. They can be seen congregating together in class, Bible studies, or in worship. They wear distinctive haircuts and special tattoos, and they communicate their camaraderie through signs and handshakes.

Volunteers are needed to help break youths' involvement with gangs. As noted in chapter 4, volunteers help youths to be honest with themselves without the worry that what they say will be used against them by the staff. As a volunteer, you can become a friend to the youths, a role model, and a surrogate parent. In a small way, you help to meet the youths' need to feel accepted and protected. You can help youthful offenders to set obtainable goals and make commitments to conventional lines of behavior. You offer encouragement and praise for the youths' achievements in obtaining goals and for choosing acceptable behavior.

You can also function as a teacher in areas where you are an expert and can fill in the gaps caused by lack of adequate funding. You can provide extra tutoring and act as a mentor for youths. You can help teach the skills necessary to attain a successful lifestyle in acceptable ways. You can work with parole officers to offer more intense supervision. When youths are released from the detention center, you can offer them the social support they will need. You can continue to provide youths with encouragement and reinforcement for their involvement in conventional activities while being someone they can trust and rely on when they are in trouble.

> Youthful offenders may be criminals, but they still possess that spark of innocence that is the image of God.

Finally, youthful offenders may be criminals, but they are still children, and as children they still possess that childlike spark of innocence, innocence that is the image of God in each individual. You can help youths to rediscover the image of God within them. You can offer juveniles role models in faith and help to instill in them a belief in moral order and a respect for the law and the rights of others.

While at the detention center, you can, with the permission of the staff, provide clothing or other necessities needed by the children. When juveniles are sent from the detention center to the long-term correctional facility, you can follow up on them by writing letters and making visits.

Two factors defeat efforts to rehabilitate juveniles. The first is the juvenile's addictions. Recidivism rates are high for juveniles who have addictions of all sorts, including smoking, drugs, alcohol, and food. Two thirds of all relapses occur within the first ninety days following release (Chaneles 88). You can encourage offenders to stick with the treatment program, which is often a condition for parole and staying out of prison, and you can help them deal with cravings for drugs and encourage them to become involved with satisfactory activities such as work and school (Dembo et al. 39).

The second factor that contributes to recidivism is institutionalization. When faced with the uncertainties of life on the street, some offenders will commit delinquent acts so that they will be arrested and sent back to the institution because it is a more predictable environment and easier for them to handle (Chaneles 17). You can attempt to improve offenders' self-esteem as a means to facilitate post-release adjustment (Vicary & Good 116).

Ministry to Incarcerated Women

Most incarcerated women are in prison as a direct result of the men in their lives. They have killed husbands or boyfriends or have become involved with them in a crime, often with only passive consent. The men ask them to do something, and they do it without considering if it is legal. The usual crime is the delivery of drugs. Drugs play a major role in the crimes committed by about sixty percent of all women inmates. Often women prisoners will accept responsibility for the crime because they believe they will receive a lighter sentence than their male partners. Many women inmates are embezzlers, thieves, and bad-check artists, but few of them are muggers and armed robbers (*Insight* [February 13, 1989]: 13). While they may be accomplices in crime, generally women are quickly forgotten by their partners once they are in prison. While wives and girlfriends crowd into visiting rooms at men's institutions, visiting days at women's prisons are virtually all-women affairs (Church 21).

Women inmates tend to be slightly better educated and less violent than men, and many of them are victims of physical violence or sexual abuse (Salholz et al. 51). Although sixty percent of the women prisoners in the federal system have been convicted of drug-related offenses such as the possession, sale, or delivery of drugs, as many as ninety-five percent are there because of drug-related crimes such as theft, armed robbery, and prostitution (Church 20). Certainly, one of the main priorities in the rehabilitation of women inmates is to help them overcome the effects of their battered pasts. Self-esteem training is essential if women inmates are to gain control over their addictions and their dependence on the men who beat them, sexually abused them, and hired them out as prostitutes. The volunteer should be especially sensitive to these issues and help women inmates to explore the violence they have experienced in their pasts and to begin to take positive steps toward healing.

Another important issue involving women prisoners is their children. A woman may be a prostitute and junkie on the street and leave the care of her children to her mother or sister, but as soon as she gets into jail, she becomes obsessed with her children. She worries about who will take care of them, but she worries even more about whether she will lose custody of them.

One woman inmate I knew worried constantly about her "kids." She constantly tried to manipulate the chaplains and other staff members to provide her with free telephone calls so that she could talk to them. Upon her release, she did not go to visit her "kids" but went straight to her local pusher and got high.

> One of the main priorities in the rehabilitation of women inmates is to help them overcome the effects of their battered pasts.

Within a few weeks, she was back in prison because she had violated her parole.

On the other hand, some women inmates who have children tend to lead quiet and docile lives in prison (Salholz et al. 51). They want to serve their time as quickly as possible and get back to their children.

Visits from children are rare because, like most prisons, women's penitentiaries are located far from urban areas and are often inaccessible by public transportation. In some areas, churches provide buses on a monthly basis so that family members can visit their incarcerated loved ones. Often PACT volunteers in the federal system will raise money for transportation so that the children of inmate mothers can come for a visit. When children do manage to visit, the prison setting can be frightening for them, and the sessions can be traumatic for both the mother and her children when the visit ends. Some institutions try to provide special visiting areas, filled with toys, for children and their mothers.

Prison authorities and volunteers who work with the children of women inmates have a responsibility to try to prevent the children of inmate parents from becoming another generation of criminals. Very often the children of inmate parents become wise to the ways of the convict. During one children's day at the Federal Correctional Institution at Fort Worth, Texas, I observed the child of one of the inmates. The child passed a clown on the prison yard who wore a painted, sad face and who walked around "crying." The child looked at the clown and said, "What's the matter? Did you lose your parole date?" While this is funny, it clearly demonstrates the child

knew the ways of the criminal justice system and probably did not have a positive opinion of it. "If the public
is wise, the children of inmates, who have never hurt
others but have only been hurt, will be gathered up into
our loving concern and taught compassion and the will
to learn, while there is still time to save them from these
hallowed halls" (Harris 252).

Another issue in women's corrections is homosexuality, but homosexual behavior among women prisoners is
different than among men inmates. While homosexuality
among male prisoners is for the purpose of sexual gratification and domination over weaker inmates, homosexuality among women prisoners is for solace and
comfort. When a woman comes to prison, she is fright-
ened and alone. She has had everything taken away from
her, and she is looking for security and affection. Female
inmates will become involved in intense schoolgirl
crushes complete with notes, love poems, and marriage
ceremonies (*Insight* [February 13, 1989]: 13). The most
notable difference between homosexuality among male
and female inmates is that females often form families.
Women of different ages will play the roles of mothers,
daughters, and aunts. Those inmates with power and
influence over others tend to take the role of parents.
Parental advice is heeded by the younger inmate because
she feels the advice is for her own good. The woman who
plays the male role, often referred to as the "butch,"
"stud," or "bull dyke," is also a leader over those who
assume the femme or female role. This division of roles
is accepted and reinforced by family members (Van
Wormer 15). For the femme, the butch can be just as

difficult as the man she left on the street and as inclined to have three or four other women she is stringing along. This is socially acceptable among the women inmates because there are many more femmes than butches. If, however, the female has more than one butch, she runs the risk of physical abuse by one or both of them (Harris 112). A butch may still show some interest in traditional female activities such as sewing and decorating her room with dolls. Blacks tend to become butches while whites become femmes (Van Wormer 15).

Homosexuality among inmates, whether men or women, is disruptive to the orderly operation of a correctional facility because of the violence it tends to breed, and prison administrators tend to discourage it. Because its practice is so widespread among women inmates, it is difficult to control. Correctional officers will try to separate butches from their femmes by moving them to different living quarters, but these women will either form new relationships or seek opportunities to be together in other situations like class, Bible study, or worship services. In these situations, the volunteer who conducts the class or worship service would do well to separate the pair by having them sit on opposite sides of the room. If they fail to comply, the officers should be notified, and the two should be ejected from the group.

> Homosexuality among inmates is disruptive to the orderly operation of a correctional facility because of the violence it tends to breed.

Another issue involving women prisoners is sexual

131

abuse by the staff. Women inmates are powerless compared to the staff, and often male staff members will take advantage of this weakness. When they fall prey to sexual abuse, women tend to be submissive and keep silent while they wait for their release date (Traxler 10). Even when they speak out, other staff members often do not believed them. I encountered one situation in which a male staff member sexually molested a woman inmate. After I got her permission to report the incident, she was placed in solitary confinement and later transferred to another institution while the staff person was exonerated. Unfortunately, the story did not end there. The staff person went on to molest other women and was eventually dismissed. It is now a federal crime for a staff person to sexually abuse an inmate. If you learn of sexual abuse, immediately report it to the prison authorities.

Ministry to women is time-consuming. Women are more vocal in expressing themselves; they talk more freely than men. They need and demand more attention than men. Women inmates do not have a code of silence like men prisoners; they complain freely about each other and the staff, and they will "snitch each other off" to staff members (*Insight* [February 13, 1989]: 13). Ministry to women can be a strain, but you will find it rewarding as you help them to gain confidence and self-esteem.

Ministry to the Condemned

The United States is the only western industrialized nation that continues to sentence capital offenders to death (Bohm vii). The goal of most death penalty legislation is the prevention of murder, and at present thirty-eight states prescribe capital punishment for various forms of homicide while the death penalty is available in a few jurisdictions for other crimes (Bailey 34). Due to the severity of the death sentence, the legal processes of review take years to decide, and condemned prisoners usually spend a minimum of six years on death row while they wait for a decision to spare their lives or, once all legal routes are exhausted, to execute them. The result is that in the states where capital punishment is enacted there is a permanent death row population (Coontz 88).

Capital punishment remains a controversial sanction for three reasons. The first is the danger of putting an innocent person to death. The second is that the sanction is applied arbitrarily. In jurisdictions like those in Kentucky, the law defines as capital offenses murders in which there are more than one victim, murders that involve a concurrent felony, murders of a law enforcement officer, and murders committed by someone with a history of convictions for violent offenses. However, prosecutors are not required to seek the death penalty in any one of these circumstances and have the discretion to file lesser charges instead (Bohm 54). The third reason is that the death penalty discriminates against minorities. In some jurisdictions, like in South Carolina, research has demonstrated that the race of the offender and victim (particularly the latter) influenced a prosecutor's decision about whether or not to seek the death penalty (Bohm 51). Blacks convicted of killing whites were more likely to receive a death sentence (Bohm 55). The future dangerous behavior of a defendant is one of the criteria used by many states in the determination of whether capital punishment is an appropriate sentence (Bohm 71).

Popular support for the death penalty has risen more than thirty-three percent since 1966 (Bohm 117). One reason proponents give for applying the death penalty is that it will prevent people who have committed the crime of murder from doing so again. Studies of death row inmates whose sentences were commuted to life when the Supreme Court overturned the death penalty in *Furman v. Georgia* in 1972 show that inmates either remained in prison or were paroled, and as parolees did better than expected. Of the six hundred inmates who were removed from death row and are now on parole, eighty percent remain free, and fewer than one percent have been convicted of another homicide. In Texas the parolees' recidivism rate of twenty-eight percent is conspicuously lower than that of the general prison population of forty-five percent (Carroll 56). Homicides committed by those released from death row have accumulated to eight citizens, one inmate, and two correctional officials. Some may argue that this constitutes an unacceptable risk, but with only eleven murders committed by a few of the released inmates, one may argue that society's protection from convicted capital murderers is not greatly enhanced by the death penalty (Bohm 96). In a fallen world, we must sometimes use force to restrain the most violent and dangerous members of society, but it is unclear whether or not the death penalty offers any real protection.

There are moral reasons for not applying the death penalty. The death penalty brings out the worst in society because it appeals to our desire for revenge rather than reconciliation. It does not restore life to the victim and only makes more victims out of the families of condemned prisoners (Metz 12). Often, after years on death row, inmates are not even the same people. They have turned away from violence and are truly repentant for what they have done.

Ministry to death row inmates is difficult. Condemned inmates are segregated from the general prison population because it is assumed that they are security risks to themselves, other prisoners, and prison personnel. They spend as many as twenty-three hours a day confined to their cells. They eat their meals in solitude and are only let out of their cells for exercise and showers. Religious services are provided once a week on an individual basis at the door to their cells. Generally, they are not allowed to work or participate in any of the programs offered to the other inmates. They have rigid restrictions placed on their visitation rights, and visitors are often separated from inmates by a panel of glass, and conversation is carried on using a telephone.

Women on death row pose a difficult problem for the states. Since so few women receive the death penalty, states do not have a specific unit or facility to accommodate them. They tend to be shifted from one institution to another or placed adjacent to units where prisoners with serious mental disorders are housed. As in most prisons, condemned women find themselves far from family, friends, and lawyers (Coontz 91). Their families have abandoned them, and their children suffer ostracism from their communities. Like other women inmates, the crimes of these women typically involved a man. Half were codefendants with their husbands or lovers. Half are mothers, and most have not graduated from high school and have limited work experience. None of them had ever killed before (Coontz 92).

Ministry to the condemned attempts to provide reconciliation and hope. Regardless of how terrible the crime, inmates can be reassured that God still loves them and is willing to forgive them. Having someone listen to their confessions and pronounce their absolution is comforting to them. They have the hope that although they are condemned in this world, they will not be condemned in the next one. They can get on with the rest of their lives. Because the appeals process takes so long, none of them, like the rest of us, really knows how much time they have left. The prison minister tries to help them to live that time as richly as possible.

The greatest challenge to ministry to the condemned is the inmates' sense of "meaninglessness." Because those on death row are so strictly confined, isolation and enforced idleness become the daily routine. The rules and

> In spite of death, the minister helps condemned inmates to find life.

regulations become a means by which extreme idleness is structured into activity, and condemned inmates organize their lives around such activity. Apparently meaningless deeds, dictated by the rules, become the focus of activity on death row. Each activity that breaks the monotony is savored by inmates in the same way a connoisseur savors a choice wine. Inmates become more aware of everything they do, from lighting a cigarette to picking up a piece of paper. On death row, people either accept the reality of death and take charge of it or go crazy (Vollers 54). In an environment of social isolation, "meaninglessness" becomes meaning (Coontz 90).

In the midst of life, we are in death, but most people have learned to give meaning to their lives in spite of death. Ministry to condemned inmates is like ministry to terminally ill patients. Death is present every minute of every day, but in spite of death, the minister helps condemned inmates to find life.

Ministry to the Insane

Ministry to the criminally insane poses special problems to the prison volunteer. Many of these people are delusional, often with religious overtones, and fixate on themes from Revelation. Some are in prison because they acted with poor judgment due to their illness. One inmate I met was manic-depressive. Before his arrest, in one of his manic phases, he thought he could do no wrong and he embezzled thousands of dollars from the financial institution for which he worked. When he was arrested, he was in a deep depression and lived as a hermit. For months he lived in his cell and refused to come out, not even to go to the television room. Another inmate had set fire to a person's house while trying to kill fire ants that had nested in the wall. Still another inmate had threatened to kill himself because he believed God told him he was the antichrist.

The trap that the untrained volunteer can fall into is to allow the mentally ill person to lead them along the path of his particular psychosis. One inmate I ministered to worked on the prison chapel detail. She was a chronic liar, a trait that had gotten her locked up. One day, she claimed that the other inmates on the prison detail were stealing greeting cards from the chapel card shop. When I had the lieutenant investigate this accusation, hundreds of missing greeting cards were discovered in her cell while none were found in the possession of the other inmates on the detail.

Work with the insane can be dangerous. When I refused to be led by an inmate along the path of his particular delusion but instead chose to have the inmate focus upon his illness, the inmate became extremely violent. This incident happened in the Dallas County Jail, and I was thankful for the glass screen between us.

Hospice

With longer prison sentences, more and more inmates grow old and die while in confinement. AIDS among drug users has introduced a new segment to the prison population. Prisons now have a group of inmates who, while healthy when incarcerated, will sicken and die while in custody. In past years, governments were inclined to release terminally ill inmates, but this practice has been greatly reduced in recent years because inmates sent home to die committed new crimes after their release, some of them quite heinous.

I ministered to one inmate who was within three months of his release date but suffered from cancer of the brain. He hoped and prayed for an early release so he would not have to die in prison. He made plans for what he would do when released and clung to every bit of news from his parole board with renewed hope, but, alas, it was not to be.

Hospice is a concept in medical care that allows the patient to die, if possible, at home and among friends and family members who provide love and care for the patient. That is not an option for most terminally ill inmates. However, several prisons have tried to provide the next best thing. The United States Medical Center for Federal Prisoners at Springfield, Missouri, and Sing Sing in New York have instituted programs in which inmates and staff are trained to work with AIDS patients. They provide individual care to the dying, bathing them, making their beds, and clothing them. They write and read letters, share the Bible or other Scriptures, and offer other personal acts that give human dignity to the dying.

| 10 |

How to Prepare

Of all ministries, prison ministry is possibly the most difficult and stressful. Many volunteers enter this ministry full of enthusiasm but soon burn out, feeling defeated and discouraged. Proper preparation is essential for any prison ministry to succeed. If you are interested in prison ministry, you would do well to begin with prayerful discernment. Prospective ministers should be prepared to get in touch with parts of themselves they have kept hidden deep within. Prison ministry will bring out feelings such as vindictiveness, anger, futility, aggressiveness, and fear. Prison volunteers will soon recognize their own capability to commit any crime describable.

A person who enters criminal justice ministry should believe in it and in his or her ability to make a difference. If you do not believe in your ministry, then the best strategy is to leave it to someone else. By prayer and communion with the Holy Spirit, you will discover if God is truly calling you to this ministry. Prayer will sustain you in times of dryness and discouragement.

If you enter this ministry, you should be aware of the competition. A person from a mainline church will find him or herself challenged by groups from the fundamentalist, evangelical traditions who believe that anyone who does not profess their particular brand of religion is not a Christian. I repeatedly have been called to defend the Catholic faith against those who claim that Catholics are not Christians. Become firmly grounded in the Christian faith and theology. Know and understand church history and tradition. Know what you believe and why.

However, avoid religious wars. Christians of every religious persuasion should emphasize the points of faith they share in common, and there are many. All Christians share faith in Jesus Christ, who saves us by his death and resurrection as revealed in the Bible. The Bible gives those who strive to be Christlike a solid blueprint for living. Christians would do well to present a united front to those who are incarcerated. The need for Christian unity and purpose is much more important in the prison setting than in any other environment (Oldham 203). Inmates are very sensitive to divisions and exploit them for their own advantage.

> Inmates are very sensitive to divisions and exploit them for their own advantage.

Next, learn as much as possible about prisons and the criminal justice system. The bibliography at the end of this book provides several good resources for beginners. Then, discover which prison ministries are active in your area. The chaplain or administrators at local correctional facilities can answer this question. Local or district church authorities may also be helpful. Select the ministry that best fulfills your interest and become involved.

However, if a prison ministry does not exist in your area, or if you are interested in establishing a ministry tailored to a specific religious denomination, more work must be done. You should first contact church officials and advise them of your desire to start a prison ministry. Attempt to get their sanction and recognition as a representative of that church body. This is important because too often people in different parishes will begin their ministries without respecting other groups who are working in the jails or prisons and attempting to coordinate their work. This lack of coordination will lead to wasteful duplication of effort and leave gaps in areas that should be covered. Then begin to contact other people who may also be interested in prison ministry. Advertise in church newspapers and parish bulletins or from the pulpit. Be certain to give clear information about places, dates, and times for meetings to organize, plan, and assign tasks.

At the first meeting, try to create a comfortable atmosphere. Provide refreshments and begin by sharing your own vision for prison ministry. Allow others to express their thoughts and record their statements on a board or newsprint so everyone can see and make comments. From these statements, the group can begin to define its goals. The goals should be clear. Vague goals like "changing the system" will not work. Like most institutions, the last priority of the criminal justice system is change. If change does come, thank God because it is the work of the Holy Spirit and not that of individuals. Goals should be specific with suggested timetables to accomplish them. Rather than aiming at doing good, the group should have the underlying ideal of doing the least amount of harm. In subsequent meetings, action plans can be established in order to achieve the goals. Also, when planning programs, remember that prison populations are in constant motion. Inmates constantly are received and discharged or moved from one facility to another. Even in long-term facilities, prison populations experience a fairly rapid turnover. For that reason, any program presented in a prison environment should be short, no more than six to eight weeks. Members of the group should work together to gather information and contact members of the community and government agencies for support.

The group must expect and anticipate setbacks. Some government agencies will be helpful, but others will be suspicious until you prove yourselves (Denton & Spitz 2). Although correctional authorities derive their authority from and are paid by society and are accountable to the society they serve, they form an impenetrable wall that divides the free society from that of convicts. Usually, they oppose any outside communication between the free world and their wards (Denton & Spitz 278).

Prison officials have good reason to be suspicious of volunteers because of problems they have had with other volunteer organizations. They see them come and go and question any new group's sincerity and willingness to stick with it. The criminal justice system desperately needs committed people who will remain consistent.

Other volunteers have given prison officials problems. Rather than entering a correctional institution with the attitude of a do-gooder, be ready to learn and ask informational questions. Above all, do not precipitate a disturbance. Many volunteers are attracted to prison ministry in order to satisfy a psychological need to associate with individuals they view as immoral or as having emotional or psychological problems, and some seek sexual contacts or criminal associations. Some volunteers see themselves as religious reformers who seek a captive audience for their high-pressure sermons and exhortations. Others see themselves as defenders of human rights who think of inmates as victims of social or economic circumstances. They view the correctional staff as overly cynical, suspicious, and security conscious and interpret security procedures as forms of cruelty or harassment of prisoners. They express uninformed opinions to the media or general public and create public relations problems for correctional officials. F. Lee Bailey once stated, "Justice is a decision in my favor." Most of the prisoners in jail do not want justice; they want out (Meyer 576). Some volunteers, in spite of the rules, bring contraband into jails or prisons. Sometimes they

> Rather than entering a correctional institution with the attitude of a do-gooder, be ready to learn and ask informational questions.

can create situations that physically endanger themselves, staff members, and inmates. Other volunteers
make grand promises they cannot keep. They raise the
expectations and hopes of inmates and disappoint them
when they fail to keep appointments or their promises
(Kratcoski 31).

When dealing with prison officials, do not be intimi-
dated. Bear in mind that prison officials are public ser-
vants paid by the public to provide a service for the public
and the prison volunteers (Denton & Spitz 9). However,
treat prison personnel with the respect any human being
deserves. Show officials that you represent a church
body and are officially recognized by it. Letters from
church leaders will help. Be clear about what you will
offer to help the prison's programs and how it will affect
the inmates. Vague statements like "We want to start a
Bible study group" or "We want to have a prayer group"
are not appreciated. Be specific about the content of the
program, the materials used, and the expected results.

Before your group begins its ministry, each prison
minister must receive proper training. Correctional staff
are well-trained professionals; you too should be well-
trained. Many correctional facilities and criminal justice
services provide specialized training for their volunteers
and inform potential volunteers of the requirements and
the dates and times for training. Others, such as the
Dallas County Jail, rely on volunteer organizations like
Prison Fellowship to provide training for their volunteers.

The burnout rate for persons working in criminal
justice is high. Volunteers working on a one-to-one basis

with criminals have different experiences, problems, frustrations, failures, or successes. Each minister should have a way to share these different impressions and reactions with each other and the staff. Meet regularly in order to vent your feelings and seek mutual support in prayer, study, and fellowship. Staff from the institutions that are served by the group should be invited to attend these meetings from time to time and be on the program agenda. They can exchange information with volunteers and discuss general and specific problems. These meetings also offer the best occasion for professional lectures on various aspects of the criminal justice system. Ex-offenders who have been served by the group should be invited to share their experiences and make suggestions for better programming. Through their participation, volunteers can benefit by witnessing some of the positive results of their work.

Finally, any organization that works in the criminal justice system should begin to think in terms of prevention: "What can my church do and what can my church be to develop the kind of resources within individual people and within the community to enable it to avoid the criminal-justice system entirely?" (Meyer 576).

| 11 |

Security, Security, and Security

Security is *the* dirty word in prison ministry, but security is necessary. As one captain liked to remind me, the people in prison did not get there by singing too loud in Sunday school. Many are a threat to society and would escape if given the chance. Others attempt to continue their criminal careers while they are locked up. The job of the correctional officers is to prevent escapes and criminal activity while keeping the inmates in a safe and humane environment. The correctional staff expects volunteers and other people who work with inmates to do the same.

Security is *the* primary concern for prison officials, and they have established numerous rules to see that security is not compromised. Your job is to learn the rules and to help prison officials maintain security.

1. Do not give anything to an inmate and do not take anything from an inmate.

This rule is simple and straightforward. It means exactly what it says, and should be easy to understand, yet I have had to dismiss several volunteers because they did not obey this simple rule. Under certain circumstances, volunteers may give things to inmates, but they should always clear it with the staff first. Under certain conditions, the staff in most prison settings will allow volunteers to give Bibles, study materials, and worship and devotional aids to inmates. Often the materials must be left with a staff person, usually the chaplain, and distributed by the staff after being checked for contraband. Sometimes, the staff will allow you to give material directly to inmates; however, you should always show the material to the staff member first and get permission every time even if the material is similar to material that has been given away before. The staff member examines the material to be certain that the material does not contain contraband and is not restricted by policy. Do not assume that because one staff member has constantly approved material for distribution another will do the same. You should always and every time receive permission before giving anything to an inmate.

2. Learn to say, "No."

Inmates will ask you for anything. If you make a promise, then find that you cannot keep it, you lose the respect of the inmate. It is far better to say, "No," ask to find out if the inmate's request can be granted, and then go ahead and do it. After a while, you will learn which requests can be granted and which cannot. People who try to help others find it difficult to say, "No." Prison volunteers want to help. They want to do good. At first, you may find it difficult to say, "No," to inmates, but with practice it gets easier.

Inmates have resources available to them. They can use the telephone and write letters. They have a medical staff available to them. They have access to a law library. Their lawyers and parole officers will visit them at the appropriate times. Encourage inmates to use the available channels of communication before attempting to help them. If inmates say they have tried this or that, check it out before charging to the rescue.

3. Dress and conduct yourself in an appropriate manner.

Women should dress modestly with blouses or dresses that cover the shoulders and dresses or slacks that cover the knees. Remember that men who have been held in confinement have pent-up sexual drives, and many criminals view women as objects for their own gratification. Women should dress in a manner that will not elicit these responses from inmates.

Men should dress in at least a shirt and slacks. A coat and tie would be even better. Men should not dress in clothing that would resemble either the uniform of the correctional staff or that of the inmates.

Do not adopt the language or mannerisms of the inmates. You are a role model. Do not criticize other volunteers, the staff, prison policy, or other inmates in the presence of the inmates. Criticisms and questions should be directed to the appropriate staff member in private. If you are having a problem with a particular inmate or group of inmates, discuss it with the staff supervisor. Inmates look for opportunities to start trouble. If they can generate divisions between volunteers and the staff, among staff members, or between individual inmates or groups of inmates, so much the better for them. If inmates cause divisions, they weaken the authority of the staff.

Always avoid inappropriate touching. A handshake is appropriate, but a hug, especially between persons of the opposite sex, is not. Women volunteers should not allow inmates to hold hands with them. They should never allow inmates to use sexually suggestive language. An inmate may comment on a volunteer's hairstyle or a particular piece of clothing; if it is a compliment, thank the inmate but get on with the subject matter of the program. If the inmate persists in his advances, tell him that the conversation is inappropriate. If the inmate continues to make advances, report him to the staff.

4. Obey the instructions and orders given by the staff.

The correctional facility is a living organism that grows and changes daily. Changes in one area or an emergency can have a direct impact on your program.

Be ready to change. You may have to change the time for the program, or the room assignment may change. Emergencies such as bad weather, disturbances, or escapes may cause you to cut short the program or to cancel it altogether.

You may work in an institution for months or years without problems and one day be asked by the staff to submit to a search. Staff members are doing their jobs, and you should submit to their requests. To do so will increase respect for you in the eyes of the staff, make life easier for all the volunteers, and help the staff to do their jobs. If you consider a request unreasonable, discuss the problem with your supervisor.

Searches are a humiliating but necessary procedure to assure the security of the institution. You might think the staff should trust you, but too often trust has been betrayed. I know of one incident in which a church group had been visiting the Dallas County Jail for months. They brought a portable organ with them. On one occasion, the staff discovered a gun hidden in the organ. Other volunteers have attempted to smuggle narcotics inside of Bibles into correctional facilities.

5. Arrive early and start and end on time.

Correctional facilities have fixed schedules for inmates to eat, work, and be counted. The correctional staff will not tolerate a volunteer making inmates wait for a program to begin. The inmates will often become irritable when made to wait, and a disturbance could result.

Likewise, staff will not tolerate a volunteer making inmates late for counts, work, or meals. Most institutions are large, with hundreds or thousands of individuals. To function efficiently, they must be kept on schedule.

6. Be patient and courteous.

The staff have their own duties and functions to perform. Often they are under-staffed. Line staff are under pressure to meet the expectations of both their supervisors and the inmates. Paperwork is a terrible burden. The staff must conduct inspections and searches, move inmates, and keep the prison clean. To meet your needs, the staff must take time out from their other duties. When the staff is busy, wait patiently until a staff person is available to help begin the program.

7. Do not give personal information to the inmates.

Do not give out your address or personal phone number. If you think it will help an inmate and have permission from the staff, give the mailing address or phone number of a church office where letters or messages can be received. Remember that you are dealing with criminals and do not want them to show up on the front porch in the middle of the night.

Do not let inmates know about your family. Wives, husbands, and children can be taken hostage. Do not let inmates know about your finances. Inmates could use the information to try to bribe you or manipulate you into doing something illegal. Do not let inmates know about personal problems.

8. Avoid personal contact with inmates' families unless given permission to do so by the staff.

Many families of inmates do not want contact with the inmates and resent prison volunteers intruding into their private lives on behalf of inmates. Do not visit the families of inmates, accept gifts or money from family members of inmates, nor conduct business with family members or associates of inmates. Such activities could involve you as an accomplice in a crime.

9. Do not take anything into the institution that you do not need.

Leave purses, billfolds, house keys, pocket knives, money, and credit cards in the trunk of the car and carry only identification and car keys into the institution. If you must take medication, bring only what you will need during the time you are in the institution.

While there are some prison volunteers who think of inmates as victims of society or the system, you must always remember that you are working with criminals. While most inmates are willing to obey the rules so that they can do their time and get out, there are a few (about two percent in any prison population) who are disruptive and often predatory in nature. Because of these few, any volunteer who enters a correctional facility is taking a certain amount of risk. For this reason, the safe volunteer is one who observes the rules.

In addition to these nine rules, the smart volunteer should observe other precautions. Learn how to use the emergency telephone alarm system. Always place an object like a table and a chair between you and the inmate. Always maintain a clear path of escape to a doorway. Know where the exits are. Never work with an inmate in a area that is unobserved by the staff. Know the name of the staff person in your area and make certain that person knows where you are. Do not leave the area without telling the staff person where you are going, even if it is only to go the restroom. If you are a volunteer who has been entrusted with keys, make certain you know the key control procedures. Never allow inmates to possess keys for any reason. An inmate can make a duplicate key from an impression of the key made in a soft bar of soap.

In spite of all safety precautions, disturbances do occur in a prison. You might be taken hostage. As unlikely as such an event might be, you must be prepared for it. The first thing you must remember in a hostage situation is that prison officials will not allow the inmates to be released in exchange for the hostage. If you are taken hostage, be prepared to wait out the situation until the inmates release you or you are rescued.

In a hostage situation, the first forty-five minutes are the most critical and dangerous. The order of the institution is disrupted, and the staff and inmates are confused about what is going on. Most of the inmates will not want any part in the disturbance and will seek to vacate the area. If pressured, they will give their support because there is safety in numbers. The turbulence of the situation will continue until the staff isolates the rioters and perimeters of control are established. In the meantime, inmates will engage in a power struggle among themselves while the inmate leaders emerge.

If you are taken hostage, remain calm during this time of instability. You may be the target of abuse, but remember that much of the abuse is not personal but really directed toward the system as a whole. Passively do what the inmates demand, except to submit to rape. You may be bound and gagged; your clothing may be taken.

When calm begins to return to the situation, listen to the inmates' demands. Make an effort to understand them and even agree with the justice of their cause. In this way, you establish a bond with the inmates, and they begin to view you as being on their side. Appeal to sympathy. Complain that the bonds are too tight. Ask for food and water and to go to the restroom. If you need medication, express that need to the inmates.

After the inmates establish their power structure and the inmate leaders emerge, the prison authorities will begin negotiations with the inmates. Do not volunteer to act as mediator between the inmates and the staff. If the staff is unwilling to meet the inmates' demands, the inmates could

> In any prison disturbance, there are two non-negotiables: to supply weapons to the inmates and to release any of the inmates.

vent their fury on you. In any prison disturbance, there are two nonnegotiables: to supply weapons to the inmates and to release any of the inmates. Other items like staff changes, programs, recreation, food, and medical care are negotiable. The prison authorities will listen to the inmates' demands and negotiate as long as hostages are not threatened. They will allow time and fatigue to wear the inmates down until they finally surrender. Force will only be used if the lives of hostages are threatened. Such a process can take days or weeks, but if you follow these simple procedures, you should emerge unhurt (though a little tired and dirty).

Another hazard in working in a prison environment is the high risk of exposure to disease. Whenever large numbers people live in close confinement, disease is a risk. In the last century, the killer of inmates was jail fever or typhus. Often epidemics of the disease broke out in the prisons and spread to the surrounding communities. Today, the diseases that present the greatest concern to prison authorities are AIDS and tuberculosis. AIDS is transmitted by the exchange of body fluids in sexual activity or by the use of contaminated needles from intravenous drug use or tattooing. Five and one tenth percent of those entering jail test positive for HIV, and, of those entering prison, three and five tenths percent test positive (Valhov et al. 1129). About three percent of federal inmates entering prison test positive for HIV. Many prison systems attempt to educate inmates about the spread of AIDS through the use of needles and sexual activity. There are some indications that the spread of AIDS occurs more slowly among prison populations than in the outside population (Baker et al. 27) The prison volunteer who has only casual contact with prison inmates should have no fear of contracting AIDS.

The disease that should concern the volunteer more is tuberculosis. According to the *Journal of the American Medical Association,* in 1988 the incidence of TB in the United States prison population was more than five times the national average ([December 15, 1989]: 3258). Like typhus in the last century, TB is a growing threat. TB is easily transmitted within correctional facilities and may also become a problem for the communities into which inmates are released. The *Journal* suggests that people having contacts with inmates be tested for TB annually and that people with positive skin-test reactions and all those with symptoms suggesting TB—coughing, anorexia, weight loss, and fever—should receive a chest X-ray within seventy-two hours of skin-test reading or identification of symptoms ([December 15, 1989]: 3259).

| 12 |

Discerning What You Have to Offer

The fact that you have read this book indicates your interest in criminal justice ministry, but at this point you may wonder what you have to offer or may feel hesitant with fear of unworthiness. Several years ago, I wanted to establish a particular Bible study program at the Federal Correctional Institution at Fort Worth, Texas. I contacted the director of Christian education for the Diocese of Fort Worth and inquired which parishes offered the program and learned that a church near the prison was offering it to their parishioners. I called the church, got the leader's name, and set up a time to meet with the team. They listened attentively and said they would consider extending their program to the prison.

The leader, an elderly lady with a generous spirit, told me about her decision. She liked the idea of having the Bible study in the prison, but she did not want to get involved in prison ministry. The next Sunday, the topic of the sermon was Matthew Chapter 27. When she heard the words, "When I was in prison, you came to visit me," she recognized the voice of the Holy Spirit and accepted her call to minister in the prison. She and several other volunteers from that church worked for many years in the prison to share God's Word with them. Many of the inmates were touched by them, and some changed their lives.

Every person has a particular gift from God that they can share in ministry. Every person has something unique to offer. It may be a particular skill or an insight into a problem.

The Southern Coalition on Jails and Prisons provides direct services to prisoners. These services include visiting inmates on death row, forming prisoner organizations that initiate lawsuits, fighting the death penalty, and lobbying for alternatives to incarceration (Rosenblatt 159). Prison Fellowship provides seminars for inmates with qualified and well-trained instructors who proclaim the Gospel without denominational bias. They use the Bible to help inmates build self-esteem and mutual support. Prison Fellowship relies on thousands of local volunteers to do its work. Its volunteers teach Bible classes, write letters for inmates, offer emotional support, help out prisoners' families, and aid ex-offenders upon their release (Rosenblatt 155). It educates the public about why prisons do not work, discusses alternatives to incarceration,

> Every person has a particular gift from God.

and responds to requests for information from policy-makers (Rosenblatt 156). Chaplain Ray's International Prison Ministry supplies books, Bibles, and greeting cards. The American Bible Society, Scripture Press Ministries, and the Billy Graham Evangelistic Association provide Bibles and a wide variety of Christian literature that contribute to the spiritual growth of inmates. Music and drama groups offer concerts and plays. These groups usually draw a sizable audience and furnish wholesome entertainment while they give a Christian witness to those who attend (Oldham 212). Some volunteers work in one-on-one relationships with inmates while others work with groups of inmates who are affiliated with denominational organizations in the outside world.

Since the foundation of the United States, volunteers have been involved in the criminal justice system. Volunteers established the night watch system in cities on the eastern seaboard, and volunteers helped maintain law and order on the western frontier. In 1841 a private citizen, John Augustus, began the probation system in the United States, and early parole programs depended upon volunteers until they became part of the formal justice system. Volunteers in the Child Saving Movement were responsible for the enactment of legislation that separated juveniles from adult offenders and created the first juvenile courts.

Today, criminal justice volunteers are motivated by the desire to help others, feelings of civic responsibility, and their religious convictions (Kratcoski 33). They offer their services in every part of the criminal justice system. They work for reform and press for changes in legislation at all levels of government. They raise money to challenge certain criminal justice practices and seek prison reform in the courts. They work to establish and maintain halfway houses, detoxification centers, refuges for runaways, and job training programs for ex-offenders. They provide counseling for offenders and their families. They assist women prisoners with care for their children, and they work with juveniles in many types of tutoring, counseling, supervision, and diversion programs (Kratcoski 31). In Lincoln, Nebraska, for example, volunteers teach classes and help with employment and educational development. They assist in public relations, prepare a monthly newsletter, and handle some clerical duties for the paid staff (Denton & Spitz 337). In Florida the Salvation Army Act allows the Salvation Army or other approved public agencies to use their facilities to provide probation supervision and service. The most important service volunteers render is to provide opportunities for friendship (Kratcoski 33).

The temptation for a new volunteer organization is to try to take on too much at once. A small organization cannot respond to all the needs and requests of prisoners during their confinement and after their release; they are just too many. Small organizations can, however, establish and maintain channels of communication with other more specialized public or private agencies or institutions to provide services beyond their own resources (Denton & Spitz 272).

This summary of all the things volunteers have to offer the criminal justice system is just part of the benefits society realizes from their service. The Bible says that if someone asks us to walk a mile with him, we should be willing to go an extra mile. Going the extra mile is the duty of criminal justice volunteers—to be the voice about criminal justice to the community. The volunteer does not go this extra mile only for reasons of compassion but out of a sense of urgency and necessity (Case 19). As volunteer citizens work within the criminal justice system, they become more informed about criminal justice issues. This in itself becomes a powerful force for change. One morning at breakfast, while I was in Huntsville, Texas, doing research at the criminal justice library at Sam Houston State University, I overheard a conversation about granting inmates time off their sentences for participation in programs. At the next table sat the chairman and several members of the parole commission. I introduced myself and was invited to take part in the conversation and was able to share my views on the subject with the commissioners.

Criminal justice volunteers have numerous opportunities to speak about criminal justice issues to concerned citizens in a variety of formats, from the informal conversation to the church group, from the civic club to the commissions and legislative committees that shape public policy. Because the volunteer is informed about the issues, he or she balances the hysteria and sensationalism of the news media and politicians. The volunteer is the community's representative who can cross the prison wall and establish meaningful and lasting relations with offenders. The volunteer acquires firsthand knowledge of prison conditions and prison life, observes the shortcomings of punishment and prevailing legislation, understands the fallacy of the criminal justice system's claim of rehabilitation, and realizes the negative attitude of the community (Denton & Spitz 267).

The criminal justice system is often a dehumanizing system that generates hopelessness in both staff and inmates. The volunteer brings a different message. Through this ministry, the volunteer shows that all people possess the dignity of children of God, who are created in his image. The volunteer is a force for reconciliation. The volunteer gives witness to the common struggle of all humanity against sin and testifies to the renewing power of God's grace. The criminal may have done despicable acts, but the volunteer can show that someone still cares about him and values him as a human being. The volunteer enables offenders to reclaim their image as children of God and to learn to walk in God's light.

The criminal justice system can be compared to a glacial mass—both change very slowly. The size of the structure and the weight of the numbers of individuals involved is staggering. When confronting this huge landscape, a person is tempted to give up in despair. The way to avoid this feeling of desperation is to look at one's own unique God-given talents—one's own experience as a human being, loved and forgiven by God, and one's ability to feel and care deeply. A volunteer brings these talents to the particular person and place where he or she is called to minister. The volunteer works with one individual at a time, realizing one small victory at a time.

Jesus calls us to be fishers of people. When a person goes out to a pond to fish, he or she does not expect to catch all the fish in the pond but only a few of them. It is the same way when we fish in a pond called prison ministry.

Glossary

administrative detention: A state of confinement in which an inmate is held because his or her classification is incompatible with the classification of other inmates in an institution or because the inmate is being held subject to the outcome of a disciplinary action.

aggravate: To add to the severity of a sentence because the crime involved a weapon or the use of deadly force.

bail: Money posted by accused persons after arrest to gain release from jail and to assure that they will appear for trial. Failure to appear will cause forfeiture of the bail. Bail is usually posted by a bail bondsman, who charges about ten percent of the value of the bail. "Bail" and "bond" are used interchangeably.

bond: See **bail.**

cavity search: (referred to by inmates as a "finger wave") A search made of the inmate's body cavities. This kind of search usually requires a medical order and is conducted by someone on the medical staff.

classification: The system used by correctional systems to assign inmates to correctional facilities and programs based on criteria such as gender, history of violence, risk of escape, education, health, and so forth.

contraband: Any item in a correctional facility illegally; an item in the possession of inmates, which they are not allowed to have. There is "hard contraband," such as weapons or narcotics, and "nuisance contraband," such as excessive amounts of food, clothing, or cigarettes.

count: Set times during the day in a prison facility when the inmates are physically counted to assure their presence. Also refers to each offense charged against a person.

custody: To have legal control over a person or property.

delinquent: A juvenile who has committed a criminal act.

detain: To hold a person pending judicial action.

detention center: A facility where persons charged with a crime (usually juveniles) are held pending judicial action.

determinate sentence: A sentence of fixed length.

deterrence: The concept that punishing a person for a crime will prevent others from committing criminal acts due to fear of being likewise punished.

down (to be down): The period of time an inmate has served, as, "How long have you been down?"

felon: A person who has committed a felony, which is a crime punishable by death or by a prison term of more than one year.

frisk: See **pat search**.

good time: The reduction of an inmate's sentence for good behavior.

hack: Inmates' name for a guard or staff person.

halfway house: A form of confinement to which persons under custody may be sent after release from prison but before they are released from confinement to enable them to reestablish connections in the free community. They live at the halfway house but find jobs and begin to search for housing in the community. Inmates reside at the halfway house until they finish their prison confinement. Failure to obey halfway house rules will result in the inmate being returned to prison.

hole: Disciplinary segregation or solitary confinement. See **segregation**.

house: The inmate's cell or living area.

incapacitation: The concept that prisons prevent criminals from continuing their criminal activities by confining them under close supervision.

incident report: (referred to by inmates as a "shot") A report by a staff member of an inmate's failure to conform to the rules. Usually results in a disciplinary hearing and sanctions being taken against the inmate.

indeterminate sentence: A sentence of indeterminate length in which persons are released from prison after they have convinced the corrections officials that they have been rehabilitated and are no longer a threat to society.

indigent: An inmate who has no funds in his or her commissary account.

institutionalization: The condition that occurs when a person is placed under the custody of an institution for long periods of time. Almost all decisions are made for the person by the staff, and the individual loses the ability to make choices and decisions that affect his ability to perform when released from supervision.

intake: The process whereby persons are received into prison.

jacket: The file that contains confidential information about a prison inmate. The file includes records about the inmate's family history, charges and sentence, conduct, medical history, and programs completed.

jail: A correctional facility that houses inmates awaiting trial or those who are serving sentences of one year or less.

jailhouse lawyer: An inmate who advises other inmates about legal matters and helps them with their appeals or lawsuits against persons in the criminal justice system.

jigger: An inmate who stands watch while other inmates engage in activities that are against the rules.

joint: The prison or place of confinement.

juvenile: A person under a specific age set by law who is not tried in a criminal court as an adult.

kite: A form used by inmates to make requests of the staff. The term comes from a brand of tobacco. The inmates used to use the wrappers off the tobacco package to write their requests.

lockdown: A situation in which all the inmates in a correctional facility are confined to their housing units either to punish them for an infraction of the rules or to quell a riot or similar disturbance.

lockup: A facility used for short-term confinement, like the cells in a police station.

mandatory sentence: A sentence prescribed by law.

misdemeanor: A crime punishable by a fine or jail sentence of less than one year.

parole: A conditional release given to an inmate who has served only part of his or her sentence. Conditions for remaining out of prison usually consist of the inmate making regular, periodic reports to the parole officer, paying an administrative fee, abstaining from illegal drugs or alcohol, not possessing firearms, and abstaining from criminal activity.

pat search: A body search in which an inmate is searched by a staff person who touches the inmate through his or her clothing. Pat searches may be conducted by staff members of either gender.

prison: A correctional facility that houses persons sentenced to a year or more.

probation: An alternative to incarceration for a person convicted of a criminal offense. The criminal does not go to prison but must submit to conditions similar to the ones for a person on parole.

rap sheet: A person's criminal record.

recidivism: The tendency of ex-offenders to commit new crimes and be returned to prison.

segregation: A type of disciplinary housing unit in a jail or prison to which inmates are assigned when they are punished for infractions of the rules. Sometimes referred to as "seg" or "the hole."

shakedown: To search an inmate or an area in the correctional institution.

shot: See **incident report**.

snitch: An inmate who reports to the staff the actions of other inmates.

strip search: A body search in which an inmate is required to undress in front of a staff person and expose all areas of his or her body for visual examination. The staff member may not touch the inmate during a strip search except to restrain the inmate if necessary. These searches are usually conducted by a staff person of the same gender. However, in an emergency, any staff person may conduct a strip search.

writeup: An incident report.

yellow sheet: See **rap sheet**.

Bibliography

Acorn, Linda R. "The Challenges of Ministering to a Captive Congregation." *Corrections Today* 52, no. 7 (December 1990): 96-107.

Ajemian, Robert. "The Sheriff Strikes Back." *Time* (March 5, 1990): 18-19.

Allen, Bud, and Diana Bosta. *Games Criminals Play: How You Can Profit By Knowing Them.* Sacramento, California: Rae John Publishers, 1981.

Allen, Charlotte Low. "The Success of Authority in Prison Management." *Insight* 5 (February 13, 1989): 8-19.

Allen, Francis A. *The Decline of the Rehabilitative Ideal.* New Haven: Yale University Press, 1981.

The American Prison: from the beginning...A Pictorial History. American Correctional Association, 1983.

Bagby, Daniel G. "A Prison Crisis Ministry: The Monthly Parole Board Meeting." *The Journal of Pastoral Care* 31, no. 2 (June 1977): 109-112.

Baker, James M. et al. "Learning to Live with AIDS in Prison." *Newsweek* 113 (February 13, 1989): 27-28.

Barrett, Katherine, and Richard Greene. "Prisons: The Punishing Cost." *Financial World* 158 (April 18, 1989): 18-22.

Bennet, James. "Sentences That Make Sense: Making the punishment fit the crime." *The Washington Monthly* 21 (January 1990): 36-49.

Bohm, Robert M., ed. *The Death Penalty in America: Current Research.* Cincinnati: Anderson Publishing Co., 1991.

Bower, B. "Mental Illness Prevails in Urban Jails." *Science News* 137 (June 16, 1990): 372.

Braun, M. Miles, et al. "Increasing Incidence of Tuberculosis in a Prison Inmate Population." *Journal American Medical Association* 261, no. 3 (January 20, 1989): 393-397.

Brevis, Harry J. "Counseling Prison Inmates." *Pastoral Psychology* 7 (February 1956): 35-42.

Brodsky, Stanley L. *Families and Friends of Men in Prison: The Uncertain Relationship.* Lexington, Massachusetts: Lexington Books, 1975.

Bullough, Vern, and Bonnie Bullough. *Women and Prostitution: A Social History.* Buffalo, New York: Prometheus Books, 1987.

Burka, Paul. "State Secrets." *Texas Monthly* 19 (June 1991): 196.

Carroll, Ginny. "Staying Clean: Life after Death Row." *Newsweek* (May 6, 1991): 56-57.

Cartledge, Paul. "The Athenian State Prison." *History Today* 40 (March 1990): 62-63.

Case, John D. "Citizen Participation: An Experiment in Prison-Community Relations." *Federal Probation* 30, no. 4 (December 1966): 18-24.

Cassler, Henry H. "The Prison Chaplain." *The Journal of Pastoral Care* 8, no. 3 (Fall 1954): 165-168.

Chaneles, Sol, PhD., ed. *Counseling Juvenile Offenders in Institutional Settings*. New York: The Haworth Press, 1983.

———. *Current Trends in Correctional Education: Theory and Practice*. New York: The Haworth Press, 1983.

Church, George J. "The View from Behind Bars." *Time* 136 (Fall 1990): 20-22.

Cohen, Bernard Lande. *Law without Order: Capital Punishment and the Liberals*. New Rochelle, New York: Arlington House, 1970.

Colson, Charles W. "Alternative Sentencing: A New Direction for Criminal Justice." *USA Today* 119 (May 1991): 64-66.

Coontz, Phyllis D. "Women Under Sentence of Death: The Social Organization of Waiting to Die." *Prison Journal* 63, no. 2 (Autumn/Winter 1983): 88-98.

Crombie, George M. "Pastoral Care of Prisoners: The Role of the Prison Chaplain." *The Australian and New Zealand Theological Review Colloquium* 22, no.2 (May 1990): 12-18.

Day, James M., and William S. Laufer. *Crime, Values, and Religion*. Norwood, New Jersey: Ablex Publishing Corporation, 1987.

Dembo, Richard; Linda Williams; and James Schmeidler. "Drug Abuse Among Juvenile Detainees." *The Annals of the American Academy* 521 (May 1992): 31.

Denton, Douglas W., and Joanne Spitz, eds. *Source Book: Citizen Action in Criminal Justice*. Arlington, Texas: The University of Texas at Arlington, 1978.

DiIulio, John J., Jr. "Governing Prisons: Managing Constitution-
ally." *Society* 26 (July/August 1989): 81-83.
————. *No Escape: The Future of American Corrections.* New
York: Basic Books, 1991.
Emery, Glenn. "Juvenile Injustice, Kids and Crime." *Insight* 6
(August 27, 1990): 18-21.
Forward, Susan. *Toxic Parents.* New York: Bantam Books, 1989.
Harris, Jean. *"They Always Call Us Ladies": Stories from Prison.*
New York: Charles Scribner's Sons, 1988.
Hart, Patricia Kilday "Jailhouse Hock." *Texas Monthly* 17 (Febru-
ary 1989): 98, 100, 102.
Harvey, Anthony E. "Custody." *Theology* 78 (February 1975):
82-90.
Hippchen, Leonard J. *Holistic Approaches to Offender Rehabilita-
tion.* Springfield, Illinois: Charles C. Thomas, 1982.
Horton, Anne L., and Judith A. Williamson, eds. *Abuse and Relig-
ion: When Praying Isn't Enough.* Lexington, Massachusetts:
Lexington Books, 1988.
Ignatieff, Michael. *A Just Measure of Pain: The Penitentiary in the
Industrial Revolution 1750-1850.* New York: Pantheon Books,
1978.
Ingle, Joseph. "Neither Do I Condemn You." *Sojourners* 7 (August
1978): 26-28.
Irwin, John. *The Felon.* Englewood Cliffs, New Jersey: Prentice-
Hall, Inc., 1970.
Jones, Arthur. "Prison chaplain chisels out 'incarceration spiritu-
ality'." *National Catholic Reporter* (October 26, 1990): 14.
Knight, Barbara B. "Religion in Prison: Balancing the Free Exer-
cise, No Establishment, and Equal Protection Clauses." *Journal
of Church and State* 26, no. 3 (Autumn 1984): 437-454.

Knight, Barbara B, and Stephen T. Early. *Prisoners' Rights in America.* Chicago: Nelson-Hall Publishers, 1986.

Kratcoski, Peter C. "Volunteers in Corrections: Do They Make a Meaningful Contribution?" *Federal Probation* 46, no. 2 (June 1982): 30-35.

Lacayo, Richard. "Our Bulging Prisons." *Time* (May 29, 1989): 28-30.

Lehrman, Karen. "Restitution: Real Fine for Criminals." *The Washington Monthly* 21 (January 1990): 38-39.

Little, Mary Gay. " Programs: Who Needs Them?" *American Jails* 1, no. 4 (Winter 1988): 24-27.

Malseed, Caroline F. "Prison Ministry Needs New Approach." *The Witness* 67, no. 6 (June 1984): 6-9.

Metz, Holly. "The News from Death Row." *The Progressive* (June 12, 1990): 12-13.

Meyer, Charles. "Getting Involved in Criminal-Justice Ministries." *Christian Century* 99 (May 12, 1982): 573-578.

Mitford, Jessica. *Kind and Unusual Punishment: The Prison Business.* New York: Alfred A. Knopf, 1971.

Morris, Deborah. "Captured By Convicts!" *Readers Digest* 137 (September 1990): 77-82.

Oldham, Edward J. "Volunteers Minister to Inmates." *Corrections Today* 50, no. 5 (August 1988): 203-212.

Oliver, John W. "To Whom Should the Prison Chaplain Minister?" *Federal Probation* 36, no. 1 (March 1972): 19-22.

Palmer, John W. *Constitutional Rights of Prisoners.* 4th ed. Cincinnati: Anderson Publishing Co., 1991.

Pederkson, Duane. *How to Establish a Jail and Prison Ministry.* Nashville, Tennessee: Thomas Nelson Publishers, 1979.

"Prevention and Control of Tuberculosis in Correctional Institutions: Recommendations, Advisory Committee for Elimination of Tuberculosis." *Journal American Medical Association* 262, no. 23 (December 15, 1989): 3258-3262.

"Prisons may be overwhelmed by HIV, or serve as models." *American Medical News* (October 19, 1990): 10.

Proelss, E. Frederick. "Reflections of the Social, Moral, Cultural, and Spiritual Aspects of the Prison Chaplain's Ministry." *The Journal of Pastoral Care* 7 (Summer 1958): 69-81.

Railsback, Tom. "Juveniles in Jail." *Congressional Record* (September 25, 1973): 31420-31421.

Rideau, W., and B. Sinclair. "Religion in Prisons." *The Angolite* (January/February 1981): 31-56.

Roberts, Linda G. "Prisoners' Rights to Free Exercise of Religion: Closing the Gap between Theory and Reality." *American Criminal Law Review* 27, no. 3 (1990): 545-581.

Rosenblatt, J. "Religious Groups and Prison Reform." *Editorial Research Reports* 1, no. 3 (February 26, 1982): 151-169.

Rothschild, Matthew. "The Crime of Politics." *The Progressive* (May 1989): 28-30.

Russell, Diana E. H. *The Secret Trauma Incest in the Lives of Girls and Women.* New York: Basic Books, Inc., 1986.

Salholz, Eloise, et al. "Women in Jail: Unequal Justice." *Newsweek* (June 4, 1990): 37-38, 51.

Samenow, Stanton, E. *Inside the Criminal Mind.* New York: Time Books, 1984.

Scacco, Anthony M., Jr. *Rape in Prison.* Springfield, Illinois: Charles C. Thomas, 1975.

Scholer, Ronni. "Inmates learn about safe sex and AIDS." *American Medical News* (February 10, 1989): 31-33.

Sellin, Thorsten. *The Penalty of Death.* Beverly Hills: Sage Publications, 1980.

Strasser, Fred. "Making the Punishment Fit the Crime...and the Prison Budget." *Governing* (January 1989): 36-41.

Strasser, Fred, and Mary C. Hickey. "Running Out of Room for Women in Prison." *Governing* (October 1989): 70-71.

Sykes, Gresham M. *The Society of Captives: A Study of a Maximum Security Prison.* Princeton, New Jersey: University Press, 1958.

Taft, Philip B., Jr. "Whatever Happened to that Ole-Time Prison Chaplain." *Corrections Magazine* 4, no. 4 (December 1978): 54-61.

Thompson, E. A. "Chaplains Help Inmates Find Freedom Behind Bars." *Corrections Today* 51, no. 1 (February 1989): 52-86.

Tilford, N. Allan. "Team Ministry in a Prison." *Ecumenism* 86 (June 1987): 25-27.

Traxler, Margaret. "Sexual Abuse of Women in Prison." *The Witness* 67 (June 1984): 10-11.

Turque, Bill. "Why Justice Can't Be Done." *Newsweek* (May 29, 1989): 36-37.

"Under the Big Top." *Time* (August 6, 1990): 29.

Valhov, David et al. "Prevalence of antibody to HIV-1 among entrants to US correctional facilities." *The Journal of the American Medical Association* 265 (March 6, 1991): 1129.

Van Wormer, Katherine S. *Sex Role Behavior in a Woman's Prison: An Ethological Analysis.* San Francisco: R&E Research Associates, Inc., 1978.

Vollers, Maryanne. "As His Date with the Executioner Nears, Joe Giarratano Says He's No Killer—And Some People Believe Him." *People Weekly* (May 28, 1990): 52-54.

Waldron, Ronald J., Peter L. Nacci, eds. *Butner Study: The Final Analysis.* Research review. Washington, DC: Federal Bureau of Prisons (June 1987): 5.

Bibliography

"Why Charles Colson's Heart Is Still in Prison." *Christianity Today* 27, no.14 (September 16, 1983): 12-16.

"A Woman Behind Bars Is Often Just Like the Girl Next Door," *Insight* (February 13, 1989): 12-13.

Wooden, Kenneth. *Weeping in the Playtime of Others: America's Incarcerated Children.* New York: McGraw-Hill, 1976.

Index

More Ministry Resources

MINISTRY TO THE HOMEBOUND
A Ten-Session Training Course
Kent C. Miller

Paper, 176 pages, 8.5" x 11", ISBN 0-89390-268-3

Build an effective home-visitation program in your community. This ten-session program will help your ministers make regular and meaningful visits to the ill and homebound and their families. Easy-to-follow, detailed session plans with reproducible handouts and worksheets are provided. Sessions include: Making a Visit, How to Be Caring, Communicating Care, Practicing the Presence of God, Active Listening, Prayer As Part of Ministry, Prayer for Wholeness and Healing, Understanding Grief, Special Challenges in Visitation, and Ministry to Dying Persons.

GRIEF MINISTRY: Helping Others Mourn
Donna Reilly Williams & JoAnn Sturzl

Paper, 232 pages, 5.5" x 8.5", ISBN 0-89390-233-0

GRIEF MINISTRY FACILITATOR'S GUIDE
JoAnn Sturzl & Donna Reilly Williams

Paper, 144 perforated pages, 8.5" x 11", ISBN 0-89390- 227-6

Grief Ministry: Helping Others Mourn fills the need for an up-to-date resource that combines spiritual and psychological insights about grief-work. It covers general aspects of grieving, empathy, communication, listening, and prayer. The authors share insights on handling difficult situations, including such special cases as suicide, the death of a baby, job loss, AIDS, and divorce.

The *Facilitator's Guide* shows how to set up a program to train grief ministers using *Grief Ministry: Helping Others Mourn* as a textbook. The guide includes group listening and role-playing exercises, scenarios for discussion, a resource listing, and useful handouts you are allowed to photocopy.

For pricing information or to order, call toll-free 1-800-736-7600 (7 a.m. to 5 p.m. PST), fax 1-408-287-8748 (24 hours), or write to:

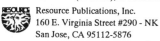 Resource Publications, Inc.
160 E. Virginia Street #290 - NK
San Jose, CA 95112-5876